Crafts of Kashmir,

Jammu & Ladakh

Edited by
Jaya Jaitly

Photographed by
Kamal Sahai

Abbeville Press Publishers New York

Editor: Ayesha Kagal
Editorial consultant: Carmen Kagal
Designer: Sunita Kanvinde

First published in the United States of America in 1990 by Abbeville
Press, Inc., 488 Madison Avenue, New York, N.Y. 10022, in
association with Mapin Publishing Pvt. Ltd., Chidambaram,
Ahmedabad 380 013 India.
ISBN 1-55859-116-8
© 1989 Grantha Corporation, 80 Cliffedgeway, Middletown, N.J.
07701.
All rights reserved under international copyright conventions. No
part of this book may be reproduced or utilized in any form or by
any means, electronic or mechanical, including photocopying,
recording, or by any information storage and retrieval system,
without permission in writing from the publisher. Inquiries should be
addressed to Abbeville Press, Inc., 488 Madison Avenue, New York,
N.Y. 10022
Printed and bound in Singapore. First printing.
Library of Congress Cataloging-in-Publication Data
Crafts of Kashmir, Jammu, and Ladakh / edited by Jaya Jaitly ;
    photography by Kamal Sahai.
        p.   cm.
    "First published in the United States of America in 1990...in
association with Mapin Publishing Pvt. Ltd., Chidambaram,
Ahmedabad...India"—T.p. verso.
    Includes bibliographical references.
    ISBN 1-55859-116-8
    1. Decorative arts—India—Jammu and Kashmir.
2. Decorative arts—India—Ladākh.   I. Jaitly, Jaya.
II. Sahai, Kamal.
NK1048.J36C74   1990
745′.0954′6—dc20   90-33198
                                          CIP

Contents

Introduction   13
Jaya Jaitly

Woven Textiles   35
Janet Rizvi

Embroidery   59
Sushil Wakhlu

Carpets   81
D.N. Saraf

Woodwork   101
P.N. Kachru and R. Thapalyal

Papier Maché   121
P.N. Kachru

Nomadic Crafts   139
Gulam Hassan Kango

Straw, Willow and Grasswork   155
Jaya Jaitly

Metalware, Pottery and Stonework   173
J.L. Bhan

Ornaments   203
J.L. Bhan and Jaya Jaitly

Glossary   220

Bibliography   225

List of places mentioned in the text

1. Akhnur C3
2. Alchi D2
3. Anantnag C3
4. Bhadarwah C3
5. Baltistan D2
6. Bandipura C2
7. Baramula C2
8. Biru C2
9. Bod Kharbu D2
10. Burzahom C2
11. Chang Thang Plains E2
12. Chengi B3
13. Chirar-e-Sharif C3
14. Chusul E3
15. Dal Lake C2
16. Demchok E3
17. Doda C3
18. Dras C2
19. Ganderbal C2
20. Haripur B2
21. Harwan C2
22. Hazratbal C2
23. Jammu C3
24. Kakhyal C3
25. Kalandarpura C2
26. Kargil D2
27. Kathua C3
28. Kishtwar C3
29. Kulgam C3
30. Lamayuru D2
31. Leh D2
32. Likir D2
33. Martand C2
34. Mulbeck D2
35. Nubra D2
36. Pahalgam C2
37. Punch C3
38. Rajauri C3
39. Raisi C3
40. Samba C3
41. Saspal D2
42. Shupiyan C3
43. Sonamarg C2
44. Sopur C2
45. Srinagar C2
46. Thanamandi C3
47. Wular Lake C2
48. Zadibal C2
49. Zaskar D3
50. Zoji-la C2

* Note :

1. Based upon Survey of India map with the permission of the Surveyor General of India.

2. Copyright 1989, © Government of India

3. The territorial waters of India extend into the sea to a distance of twelve nautical miles measured from the appropriate base line.

4. Responsibility for the correctness of internal details shown on the main map rests with the publisher.

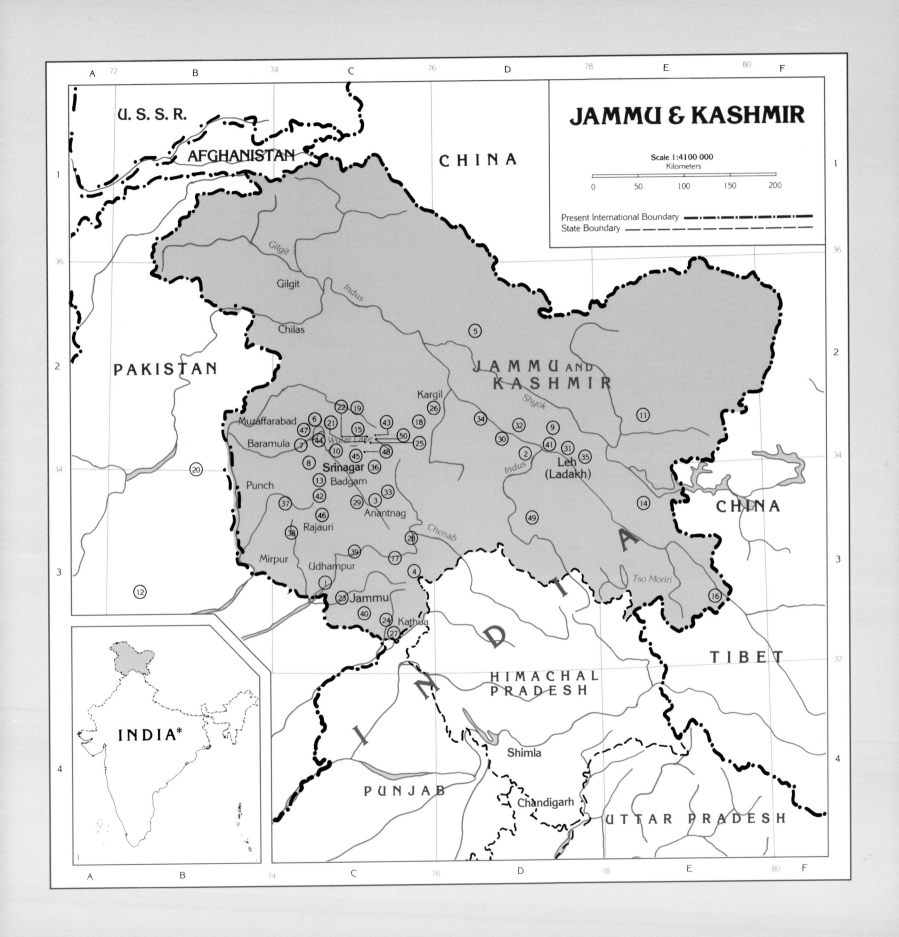

Introduction

As men and women rested from the search for food, they began to fashion tools, weave straw and yarn, mould clay and carve stone and wood. Finally, this process that began many thousands of years before Christ has evolved today into a highly complex web of science, art and technology. While this has reduced drudgery and expanded people's knowledge of the world, it has at times brought about the destruction of those very manifestations of nature which gave them sustenance.

In some parts of the world, however, the rhythm of life has set its own pace and the gentle relationship between people and nature has been maintained. One such area is the state of Jammu and Kashmir, where the crafts reflect, in equal measure, its history, landscape and way of life. A multi-racial and diverse land consisting of three distinctly separate regions, Jammu, Kashmir and Ladakh is a composite of many peoples, languages and religions, climates and cultural systems. Each region has had its share of turbulent historical events which were intertwined with those of Soviet Turkestan and Sinkiang in the north, Tibet in the east, and Afghanistan, Pakistan and Europe in the west.

These events have always been linked to the fate of artisans and the crafts. The economy of the state was also interlinked with their flowering as well as their decline.

Legend has it that *satisara*, the sea of Sati, once covered the entire valley of Kashmir. Sati was Lord Shiva's wife, otherwise known as Parvati. An ascetic, Kashyapa, prayed to the gods that the sea should dry up and when his prayers were granted the area came to be known as Kashmir from Kashmira — the lake of Kashyapa.

Archaeological and historical evidence of the neolithic settlements in Burzahom in Kashmir which are assigned to the period between 2300 and 1500 B.C., indicate that these were the earliest inhabited areas of the valley. The neolithic settlers made their pottery by hand in grey, dull red, brown or buff with a burnished surface. The items consisted of dishes, bowls, funnel-shaped vases and globular pots and jars. Some pots have a mat-impressed design which shows that grass — mat weaving was also carried out during the same period. Tools such as mace heads and hand axes were made of stone and bone. In Jammu, evidence of primitive man is available from stone age tools and pottery unearthed at Akhnoor and Ambaran.

All subsequent movements of peoples from the Middle East and Central Asia — the Aryans, Greeks, Mauryans, Kushans, Huns, Jats, Gujjars, Persians, Pathans, Rajputs and the British — through the mountains and green valleys of the region, left a varied texture of influences behind.

In the third century B.C. the great Mauryan Emperor Ashoka sent Buddhist missionaries to Ladakh and Kashmir where they established their first town, Srinagar. Kashmir became the base from where great works of Buddhism and scholarly Sanskrit literature spread and the region evolved as the crucible of a highly civilised cultural expression where Buddhism, Shaivism and Sanskrit learning flourished.

The earliest mention of Ladakh is probably in Pliny's *Cesi* in which he writes of a region *"hos includit Indus montium corona circumdatos et solitudinibus"* (The mountain range includes those which surround the Indus and are marked by desert land). This seems to accurately describe the people of Kha-Pa-Chan or Snow Land referred to by the Chinese pilgrims Fa-Hien and Hoei-King in

A.D. 399-400. Nestling amidst the massive Karakoram ranges to the north-east and the great Himalayan range to the south, Ladakh is the largest district in India today, spreading across 119,820 square kilometres. Situated 3,000 to 5,000 metres above sea level, it is sealed off by high passes of snow in the winter. Bounded by Sinkiang in the north, Tibet in the east and Gilgit in the west, Ladakh is divided in half by the Indus, one of the 20 longest rivers in the world, and is spread over the Nubra and Zanskar valleys, Kargil, a part of Baltistan, and Suru up to Dras which lies on the road connecting it to the Kashmir valley.

The landscape in Ladakh is stark, barren and majestic. The images that meet the eye are rocks, dusty plains and the odd inhabitant or sheep moving about like tiny specks across an isolated and deserted world. Beside the river tracts, fertile strips of land are cultivated with barley and wheat, and apricot groves and mud-brick houses are scattered below towering cliffs. Wisps of smoke rise from these dwellings and the people move about their work with an air of gentleness and tranquillity. There are many who sense a certain spiritual as well as terrestrial luminosity in the atmosphere.

The first inhabitants of Ladakh, one of the highest inhabited places on earth, were nomadic shepherds who lived in black animal skin tents. And even today, a traveller comes across the almost ethereal images of such encampments spread across the Changthang plain up to Demchok. The Ladakhis cover their tents and themselves with yak hair and drink thick tea flavoured with yak butter.

In Ladakh the Chiang tribes, who once roamed the pastures of Central Asia and later became settled farmers, practised an animist form of religion called Bön-pa which was rich in rituals and superstitions, spirits and demons. Despite the Buddhist missionaries sent by Ashoka, it was only when the Tibetans conquered Ladakh between the seventh and tenth century A.D. that Tibetan and Indian cultural influences began to change the essentially tribal culture into a feudal one. In the second century A.D., it was part of the Kushan empire, and the documented history of Baltistan indicates that before the tenth century A.D. Chinese, Tibetan and Kashmiri troops crossed the terrain over and over again in search of conquest and plunder.

Previous page

Herd of sheep at Zoji-la

The majestic gateway to Central Asia, Zoji-la is the high mountain pass dividing Kashmir from Ladakh and remains snow-bound for more than six months in a year. Only the nomadic Gujjars and Bakarwals venture to negotiate the icy slopes. The glistening snows and awesome mountains of the region are part of the psyche of its people.

Gujjar woman between Jammu and Kashmir

In the late spring the nomadic Gujjars move from the plains of Jammu to the mountain pastures of Kashmir, taking a week or ten days to complete the first lap of their journey which follows a fixed route. At night, they set up camps on the slopes along the roadside and women prepare the evening meal. Their distinctive silver jewellery and style of dress sets them apart from the settled population.

Tibetan culture was associated with religious and liturgical aspects. It was replete with sacred symbols, *thankha* paintings and iconography connected with Vajrayana Buddhism, which was in turn closely linked to the flourishing Buddhist centres in India. Old writings, however, make no mention of the crafts or artistry of the local people. This was perhaps because Buddha's teachings centred around the monastery and called for learning and simplicity in all aspects of life. As the historian D.D. Kosambi points out, a person's needs were minimal, restricted to "a begging bowl, a water pot, at most three pieces of plain, unembroidered patternless cloth (preferably pieced together from rags) for wear; oil, jug, razor, needle and thread and a staff".

By now Kashmir and Ladakh had become historical trading centres in the heart of the Asian continent. They served as gateways between the Punjab and the Indo-Gangetic plain and lay on the Silk Route of Central Asia. Traders from Khotan, Yarkand, Kashgar and other trading posts between China and the Mediterranean passed through here. The caravans of merchants traded in silk, shawl wool, carpets, spices, silver, turquoise, salt, tea and tobacco, creating a rich interlocking of commodities. These trade routes became passageways for cultural movements enriching the minds and the sensibilities of its people.

An example of the adorning of a heritage is seen in the moulded brick tiles of the apsidal temple and surrounding courtyard at Harwan near Srinagar, which dates back from the third to sixth century A.D. Free from the influence of any other known school, the Harwan tiles depict the life of man and nature. Motifs consist of aquatic plants from the lakes of Kashmir, lotus flowers, flying geese, fighting cocks and rams, cows, suckling calves, elephants, deer, archers on horseback and many other figures in various aspects of activity. Apart from these, there are designs consisting of frets, wavy lines, fish-bone patterns as well as the conventional flowers and leaves. The sophistication of these art forms indicates patronage of the nobility of that period. What is remarkable is the continuance of these motifs as inspiration to both the urban and rural crafts of Kashmir although their originators were people who came from Central Asia and later settled in Kashmir.

Far left
Woman selling fish, Srinagar, Kashmir

The ornamental band under the *kasaba* or square head cloth, the fish and the ring on her finger shine equally in the early morning sun as the woman unfolds her wares carried in a willow basket.

Women in traditional·attire, Leh, Ladakh

It is considered mandatory for Ladakhi women to wear the *tibi*, the *lokpa* and *tunglag* in order to be both civilised and fashionable.

The *tibi* is worn by both sexes and is a hat made by stretching sheep skin, *tsaru*, over a wooden mould and covering it with silk. It is sometimes embroidered with silver or gold metallic thread. The *lokpa* is made of sheep skin and worn attached to the shoulders with the skin turned inwards. On festive days, the *bok* is worn in place of the *lokpa*. It is made of either Benares or Kalimpong brocade or is brightly embroidered with multi-coloured tassels stitched to the edge.

Tunglag are white conch bangles made by the *gara*. The bangles of both hands are knocked together as a form of ceremonial greeting. The *goncha* or gown made of hand-woven or velvet cloth is always in dark colours — maroon, black or navy blue with a bright cloth tied around the waist. All important garments, accessories and ornaments worn by women are made by men.

Previous page

The grave of Emperor Jehangir between Rajouri and Nowshera, at Chingis, Jammu

The ancient Mughal route passed through Kashmir via Shupiyan to Noori Chhamb, (where the famed Empress Noor Jehan was said to take her bath amid sylvan surroundings), to Thanamandi via Nowshera to Lahore, now in Pakistan. It was while journeying along this imperial route that Jehangir died. It is said that for political reasons Noor Jehan did not wish this fact to be revealed before she reached Lahore and ordered that his intestines be removed to preserve the rest of the body until then. The intestines were buried at one of the traditional resting places en route which was subsequently named *chingis* or entrails. Thus while Emperor Jehangir's official burial took place at Lahore, a solitary monument to his entrails stands at Chingis in the Jammu region of the state.

Far left

Metal worker repairing brass vessels, Jammu

The Jain Bazaar of Jammu was the centre of all activity for metal workers. Today a handful remain, providing vessels for ceremonial occasions or repairing and fashioning small cooking pots in brass and copper.

Fateh Kadal, or Third Bridge, Srinagar

The hub of craft activity is still in the narrow lanes and crowded *mohallas* of the old city of Srinagar which was established by the Mauryan Emperor Ashoka around the third century B.C.

The third of seven bridges over the Jhelum river, the original Fateh Kadal was washed away in a flood soon after this photograph was taken. On either side there are many *karkhanas* where carpet weaving, *numdah* making, chain stitch embroidery and jewellery making are carried out. Wholesale dealers in handicrafts also have their showrooms and offices alongside in old wooden buildings with large, overhanging balconies. Mosques and shrines surround the busy craft activity of the Fateh Kadal locality.

Alchi Monastery, Ladakh

Incidental wall decoration and clay sculptures below the main altar at Alchi are surrealistically highlighted by rays of sunlight seeping into the chapel. These are more recent additions and embellishments to the near 1000-year old monastery which is a repository of Himalayan art in which Kashmiri artists enriched Ladakh's religious structures.

Far right

Lamayuru monastery, Ladakh

One of the oldest and largest monasteries in Ladakh, Lamayuru lies amidst a landscape of fantastic rock formations, relics of a time when a lake inhabited by mythological serpents was said to have filled the valley. Fine fern-like fossil imprints are still visible on roadside rocks.

Ladakh is one of the few areas today where Tibetan Buddhism is practised and every village has its own monastery. The two lamaist sects are known as *Nyingmapa* or Red Sect, the colour being associated with strength and power. The *Gelugpa* or Yellow Sect relates the colour to purity and spiritual elevation.

Lamayuru was built to honour the memory of a tenth century sage, Naropa, and is the ancestral seat of the Dogunk-pa, a branch of the Red Sect from Central Tibet. Over the years, the lamas expanded the monastery and decorated its interior with elaborate frescoes and statues in wood and gold inlaid with precious stones.

In Jammu, the fourth century stone temples of Sudha-Mahadeva and the fine sixth and seventh century terracotta heads of Buddha and Bodhisattvas, with their wonderfully delicate facial expression, establish the high quality of Dogra craftsmanship. The *Natya Shastra*, an ancient classic on drama and dance, was written in Kashmir between the 10th and 12th centuries. During King Harsha's reign in the 12th century, the famed historian Kalhana recorded in Sanskrit verse the *Rajatarangini*, or River of Kings, which enumerates the long succession of kings from Ashoka to Kanishka who died in A.D. 144. The massive work touches on all aspects of life — social, political, scientific and artistic — and is a rich and spectacular storehouse of information.

Later chronicles intended to continue Kalhana's work were the *Rajatarangini* of Jonaraja who wrote of events up to the reign of Zain-ul-Abadin and the *Rajatarangini* of Srivara, contained in four books, covering the period 1459 to 1486. The fourth chronicle, *Rajavalipataka*, by Prajyabhatta, extends to the time of the annexation of Kashmir by Akbar in 1586.

According to a Persian history of Kashmir, political power was founded in Jammu in A.D. 900 and it was an important entity in this hilly region even before the Turkish invasion of north-west India. Jammu's traditions and cultural influences were linked to Punjab and the Indo-Gangetic plain and the robust character of its people survived the onslaught of many tribal invasions. In the valley, after the Ephythalites led by Mihirakula had passed through, Hinduism was restored to Kashmir by the Karkota dynasty. Soon after A.D. 733 King Lalitaditya Muktapida of Kashmir defended the Dards and Tibetans. He was a generous patron of Buddhist culture and the oldest monastery in Ladakh dates back to this period. The Karkota dynasty gave a strong impetus to art and architecture in this region. Huge structures, *stupas* and temples were built all over the Kashmir valley, of which the imposing Sun Temple at Martand is one of the few that still remains.

A spate of temples was constructed to glorify the revival of the ancestral faith, but by 1338 the Hindu ruler Udaiana Deva was put to death by the Muslim grand vizier Amir Shah, who then ascended the throne as Shams-ud-din and was the first ruler of

the Sultanate period. Kashmir was once again under the influence of Islam.

In 1398 when India was invaded by Tamur Lane, Sultan Sikander sent his son to pay tribute to the invader. Tamur Lane betrayed the agreement of his alliance with Sultan Sikander and kidnapped his son Shahi Khan. This young man remained a hostage in Samarkhand for seven years where he saw the finest artists and craftsmen of China, Turkestan and Persia who had been brought by Tamur Lane from various countries held under his sway. Neither the artists nor the young prince were allowed to leave the city but Shahi Khan was free to move about among the craftsmen. He was greatly influenced by what he saw and the idea of promoting the growth of highly sophisticated forms of craftsmanship grew in his mind. When his father Sikander died he ascended the throne in 1421 as Zain-ul-Abadin and by sending for craftsmen from Central Asia and Arabia he set about building the strong foundations of organised and exquisite craftsmanship that was to make Kashmir famous the world over.

Zain-ul-Abadin introduced the art of paper making which led to the furthering of excellence in calligraphy and papier maché, skills which he imported from China and Persia. Firearms, which led to the refinement of metal work, were first introduced during his reign. He established the rearing of mulberry trees and silkworms and promoted the silk industry by inviting weavers from Kurasan. Thus, all types of skilled artisans came into Kashmir and prospered through his efforts to enrich the arts. While these forms of art and culture were brought in from other lands, a strong, indigenous tradition of weaving, pottery, stone work and jewellery-making existed alongside, interacting and often fusing with these outside influences. The Great Badshah, as he was popularly called, ruled from 1421 to 1472 and was considered the precursor of the Mughals and was known as the Akbar of Kashmir.

The Mughal era had a strong cultural and aesthetic influence on Kashmir. The *Ain-i-Akbari*, or Institutes of Akbar, speak of the Emperor Akbar's great fondness for shawls, and his wardrobe was well-stocked with them. He also introduced the idea of folding shawls length-wise and draping them around the neck as well as wearing shawls in pairs, *doshala*, by stitching them back to back so that the

underside did not show. The *Ain-i-Akbari* also tells of these exquisitely soft "cashmeres" which were already well known as gifts that reached distant lands. The Italian traveller Pietro della Valle writes in 1623 that the *scial* or shawl of Persia was a girdle, whereas in India it was generally worn over the shoulders. The rough-textured home-spun and woven shawl kept the village peasant warm while the finer pieces adorned nobility, reaching the shoulders of Josephine Bonaparte by 1798. Later, quoting early records of the East India Company, John Irwin describes how embroidered and ornamental shawls were often mentioned as useful articles of bribery.

When the Mughal Emperor Jehangir appointed Ahmed Beg Khan to govern Kashmir in 1615 a merchant called Akhum Rehnuma became involved in the manufacture of carpets. Large-scale production of carpets was undertaken in the reign of Akbar but it was Akhum Rehnuma who introduced the skill of carpet knotting to Kashmir. This was after his pilgrimage to Mecca after which he had halted in Persia, to purchase equipment and bring weavers back with him. Although the weavers in Kashmir were still deeply involved in shawl weaving, the subsequent breakdown of trade in the 19th century, due to mechanisation and the Franco-Prussian war, compelled them to turn to carpet weaving as an industry.

Around 1675 the history of Ladakh took a different turn. The Tibetans invaded the region using the religious issue of a quarrel between the Red Sect of Tibet and the Yellow Sect of Ladakh. The latter were defeated. When King Delek Namgyal appealed to the Mughal governor of Kashmir, Aurangzeb went to Namgyal's aid and successfully turned back the Tibetans. In return for his assistance, however, he demanded that Ladakh's market and fine *tus* wool be made available to Kashmiri merchants. This was also the beginning of the acceptance of Islam in Ladakh.

The Dogra land of Jammu, achieved its greatest glory during the reigns of Dhruv Dev and Ranjit Deva which is reflected by the vitality of its folk tales and martial songs. During Sikh rule, between 1819 and 1846, the high level of art patronage led to the Jammu, Basohli, Ramnagar and Kangra styles of miniature painting. It also exercised great influence over the *kani* shawl of Kashmir in terms of design and colour. During this period, the linking of the

Silk thread shop, Zainakadal, Srinagar

This establishment selling thread for embroidery, near the famous Shah Hamdan mosque, is similar to hundreds of such small, local enterprises that have been traditionally available to the embroiderer who is consequently well provided with raw materials for the pursuit of his work and aesthetic requirements. Silk, cotton and woollen threads in all hues from pastels to deep wood browns are available in shops in every locality where embroidery *karkhanas* flourish. Fine threads decorate shawls and garments while thicker woollen threads are used to embroider floor coverings and furnishing fabrics.

three regions took place in the nature and characteristics of the shawl. Apart from international inputs, the shawl obtained its fine yarn from the high-altitude goat of Ladakh, its skill from the nimble-fingered Kashmiri weaver and its exuberant new hues from the Sikh rulers of Jammu.

In 1819 Ranjit Singh, King of Lahore and member of the Sikh confederation, invaded Kashmir and pushed the Afghan forces out of the territory. Ladakh and Baltistan were unable to retain their independence and in 1833 became subject to the empire of Ranjit Singh's son Sher Singh and represented by Gulab Singh.

The famous treaty of Lahore and Amritsar concluded in March 1846 recognised Gulab Singh as an independent sovereign and Maharajah of Jammu. Item 10 of the deed states, "Maharajah Gulab Singh accepts the government of Great Britain and from his side as a gift will give every year one horse, twelve goats (six male and six female) and three pairs of *jamawar* shawls". The *kani* shawl thus became part of a document in history.

Thus, an incredibly diverse group of people — including Indo-Aryan Kashmiri Muslims and Hindus, the Buddhists, Champa and Dard Turanians and the Aryan tribes of Hindu Dogras, Muslims, Chibhalis, Paharis, Gaddis and Muslim Gujjars — constitute the population of the state. The community of Gujjars who inhabit the lower hills and plains south of the Panjal range and the Bakarwals continue their nomadic existence till today. They travel freely with their flocks of thousands of sheep and goats between the Punjab, Jammu, Kashmir, Ladakh and Pakistan, respecting no state, regional or national boundary except the border with Tibet.

The integration of Kashmir followed a few months later when the Dogra king Gulab Singh was able to prevail upon the British to sell him Kashmir for ten million rupees against the indemnities owed to them by the Sikhs. This completed the formation of the state which finally acceded to the Republic of India in 1947.

As anywhere else, while diverse people carry on different trades, the farmer often supplements his income through artisanship.

Walter R. Lawrence, Settlement Commissioner for Jammu and Kashmir, wrote in 1890: "The Kash-

Sun Temple; stone; eighth century, Martand, Kashmir

Built in the reign of King Lalitaditya around A.D. 750, the massive and bold outlines with fluted pillars and imposing colonnades was the work of skilled artisans brought by the king after his conquests in India and Central Asia. Many grand edifices were built during this period.

There are 84 columns which, the famed chronicler and Settlement Commissioner Walter Lawrence says, "is a singularly appropriate number in a sun temple, if, as is supposed, the number 84 is accounted sacred by the Hindus in consequence of its being the multiple of the number of days in the week with the number of signs in the zodiac".

There are richly carved panels and sculptured niches of Hindu deities all around the central rectangular courtyard.

Detail of *kani* shawl, *gul-e-anar* design, Kanihama, Kashmir

The famous *kani* shawl is an integral part of the history of Kashmir. At one time there were more than 30,000 looms; now there are six in the tiny village of Kanihama where young men are being trained. It takes two weavers three months to complete a shawl during training, by which time they learn the *talim* of 16 designs.

Far right

Nomadic tribe of Bakarwals, Pahalgam, Kashmir

Forever on the move to greener pastures, selling milk and *ghee* as they go along, the nomadic Bakarwals of Jammu and Kashmir migrated from the Punjab and are believed to have been part of the original Huns who spread across India. Their woollen *chadars* are woven by Kashmiri weavers, their shoes are made by *mochis* of Rajouri and their jewellery by goldsmiths in Kathua. The embroidery on sacks and blankets done by nomad women reflects influences of Punjab, Himachal Pradesh and Kashmir.

miris have won a great reputation as artisans, and were celebrated in the old days for their skills in art manufactures." He praised the skill and products of the industrious village craftsman but went on to remark upon the lack of application and ambition in his city counterpart. Till now, these craftsmen — the village potter, blacksmith, weaver and carpenter — continue to provide for the needs of the rural areas while trade crafts in the city are organised under master craftsmen, *ustads*, generally in the *karkhana* or workshop system.

While the earlier craftsmen of Jammu seemed to have developed as pure artists and sculptors attached to the feudal court and left behind extraordinary treasures in the Akhnoor carved stone and later in the ornamented Basohli paintings, the everyday artisan has remained linked to the rustic agrarian and mountain economy. The peasant is often the artisan, and communities of artisans produced goods for the local population extending to Sialkot, now in Pakistan.

In the narrow, winding Moti Bazaar of Jammu city, named after Maharajah Moti Singh, metal workers lined the street, hammering vessels into shape, repairing old urns and silver-plating dishes. Today, only two workers remain, yet the large vessels they produce are not only used in the village homes but are a necessary part of every ceremonial occasion. In tiny villages dotted across this narrow semi-mountainous region women make tasselled ornaments to bind their hair while men weave fine *nadas* or cord with which to tie their pyjamas. Earlier *nadas* were so firm and net-like, it is said, that Maharajah Pratap Singh used his to draw a bucket of water from a well while on a journey. These cords are used in Punjab, Jammu and Pakistan even today.

In Ladakh, while some communities such as the *gara* are exclusively blacksmiths, in every home men and women spin yarn — the women spin sheep's wool while the men spin the wool of the yak and goat. The division of work among the sexes in Ladakh is interesting for, until recently, there was a taboo against women handling grain. The ancient Greek belief of relating fertility and the monthly cycle of women to the fecundity of the earth also existed here. As in Kashmir, Ladakhi women traditionally do no weaving although women do so in the neighbouring regions of Nepal, Spiti and Tibet. All the artifacts worn or carried

Spinning among rural peasantry, Anantnag, Kashmir

Spinning and weaving are closely related to the life of the Kashmiri farmer. While carrying on with household or agricultural chores women continue to spin yarn. Men weave heavy *chadars* during the cold winter months when outdoor activity is restricted.

The *charkha*, or spinning wheel was made on a lathe by a wood carver as a gift for his wife. Each spoke is decorated with five wooden rings which clatter musically as the wheel turns.

by women in Ladakh, such as the *perak, goncha* or basket, are made exclusively by men.

The artisan in Ladakh sells his labour, skill and time to his customer who provides the raw material and perhaps even a meal. The price of an object is assessed by the number of days it takes to make — two and a half days for a length of woven cloth, three days for a window or for a *perak* and perhaps only two days for a pair of shoes. Objects in Ladakh are therefore largely custom- or home-made, and the few artifacts that are available in the Leh bazaar are a recent economic development.

Today, apart from the usual incursions made by machine-made goods and the march of progress which floods synthetic gadgetry into village markets, it is still the mud pot, the home-spun shawl, the *kangri* or wicker and clay chafing pot, and the glittering copper tea kettle that are a conspicuous part of the village home.

In Jammu, Kashmir and Ladakh it is the trees and flowers, the awesome mountains and the eternal snows that have consistently stirred the consciousness of the creative craftsman. The kingfisher, *bulbul* and the honeybee quicken the woodcarver's fingers while the shimmering waters of the myriad lakes and streams lend inspiration to his quest for harmony in colour and form. A deep and binding relationship with the land, encompassing its dust, soil, rock, stone and animals — whether mountain goat or valley deer — still sharpen and heighten the artistic awareness of the craftspeople.

Thus, during the chequered course of history when kings and military leaders plundered and built, created and destroyed, the common artisans and simple peasants continued to produce articles for everyday use. They reaffirmed and reiterated their dependence on the materials offered by the land around them, and the source of their inspiration was always the combination of their own needs, skills and an aesthetic response to their surroundings. This relationship between people's spiritual and creative selves and the environment in which they live is vital, for if each gives and receives in fair measure and understanding from the other the cycle of life becomes a smooth uninterrupted process — productive, self-replenishing and rich.

Village artisan and shop keeper, Kathua, Jammu

While making *hukkas* and sometimes toy bows and arrows, the rural craftsman also sells the wares of the potter and paper garland-maker in the local bazaar.

Far right

Buddhist prayer flags, Fotula, Ladakh

At various high points across the stark and majestic landscape, coloured flags flutter in the chill breeze. The prayers on them are believed to be transmitted through the air to the gods.

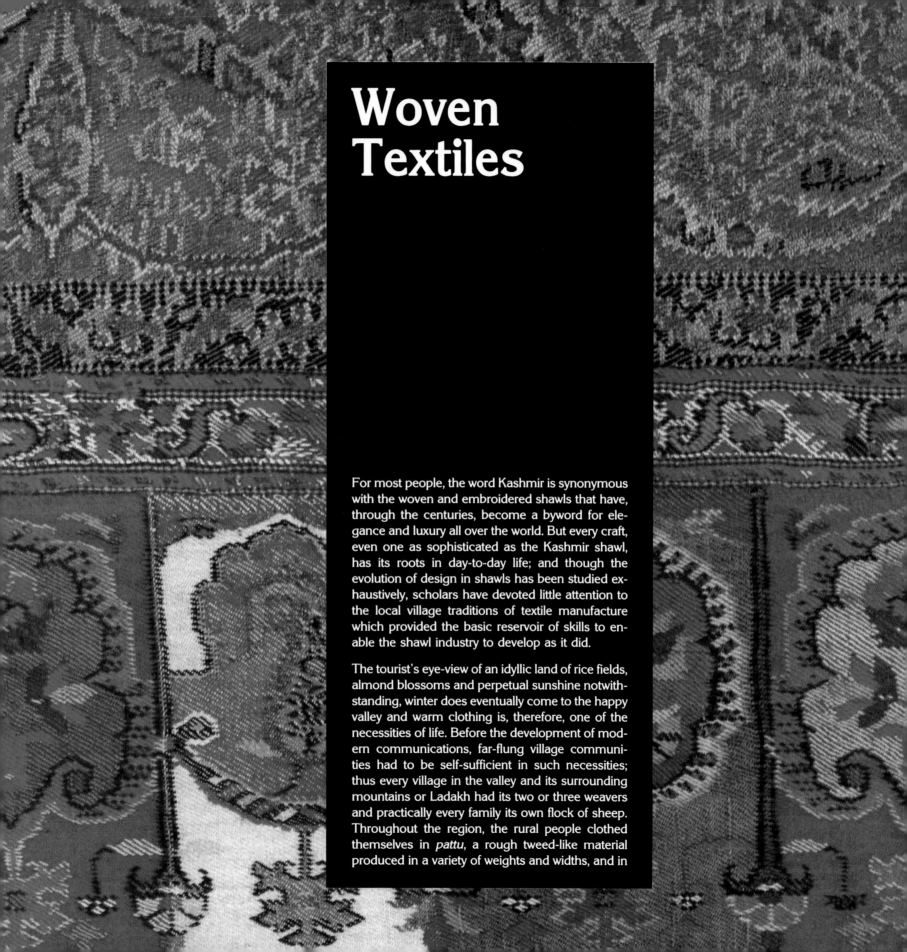

Woven Textiles

For most people, the word Kashmir is synonymous with the woven and embroidered shawls that have, through the centuries, become a byword for elegance and luxury all over the world. But every craft, even one as sophisticated as the Kashmir shawl, has its roots in day-to-day life; and though the evolution of design in shawls has been studied exhaustively, scholars have devoted little attention to the local village traditions of textile manufacture which provided the basic reservoir of skills to enable the shawl industry to develop as it did.

The tourist's eye-view of an idyllic land of rice fields, almond blossoms and perpetual sunshine notwithstanding, winter does eventually come to the happy valley and warm clothing is, therefore, one of the necessities of life. Before the development of modern communications, far-flung village communities had to be self-sufficient in such necessities; thus every village in the valley and its surrounding mountains or Ladakh had its two or three weavers and practically every family its own flock of sheep. Throughout the region, the rural people clothed themselves in *pattu*, a rough tweed-like material produced in a variety of weights and widths, and in

winter they wrapped themselves in blankets, *cha-dars*, of a number of different designs, each characteristic of the area where it was made.

Unlike weaving, which was somewhat specialised work carried on by only a few families, the craft of spinning was — and is — done by the womenfolk of virtually every rural household in the mountainous regions of Jammu and Kashmir. In Kashmir proper, indeed, the usual connotation of the word "homespun" to imply something rough and coarse though serviceable, is entirely inappropriate; for as A.F. Barker noted half a century ago in *The Cottage Textile Industries of Kashmir*, the village weaver has at his command probably the finest hand-spinning skill in the world — surpassed only by the pashmina spinners of Srinagar. The Kashmiri spinning-wheel, *yender*, has a traditional and unique design, and the one used today does not differ from the one described by William Moorcroft in 1823. There still remain places, however, where the spinning-wheel is unknown and where yarn is spun on a hand-spindle — known as *tikli* in Ladakh, where its use is universal.

In the whole of Kashmir and Ladakh, weaving is exclusively man's work though it is not a full-time occupation nor confined to a particular community like other skilled occupations, for example, carpentry or metalwork. Weavers are ordinary farmers who spend the long days of summer working in their fields, but who also exercise this hereditary skill largely in the winter months. During this time they make cloth for their own and their families' use, and also do so as a village service on payment, taking in their neighbours' yarn and returning it to them in the shape of *pattus* or *chadars*.

There are a number of different types of looms used in Jammu and Kashmir, none of them unique. The portable loom of Ladakh, for instance, has its counterparts in other mountain regions like the eastern Himalayas and as far away as the Peruvian Andes. Its special feature is that it can be dismantled and reassembled within minutes at any convenient spot, for in Ladakh's dry, sunny climate weaving is invariably done out in the open.

Since the Kashmir winter, with its overcast skies and heavy snow, does not allow for sustained out-of-doors work, everywhere but in Ladakh, looms are set up inside the weaver's homes. The old type was usually a pit-loom, though

Previous page

Detail of *kani* shawl; probably 1860s; School of Designs, Srinagar

Here the cone has been reinterpreted as a tree — a revision of one of its suggested origins. The outmost border is a typical example of the art of the *rafoogar*, the sewer of fine seams. As shawl design became more complex, from about the fourth decade of the 19th century, many of them were woven in a large number of separate pieces which were then joined together by seams of such delicacy as to be almost invisible. The report that some shawls consisted of 1,500 pieces may be exaggerated, a realistic estimate may be 15 to 20, exclusive of the border which, if composed of particularly narrow strips as in this example, might at most account for another 100 or so.

Far left

Srinagar village *chadars* as they are worn

The heavy *chadars* are a wonderful, multipurpose invention which serve as bedding, as a voluminous over-wrap in cold weather and when worn-out are recycled by a process of milling or felting into a kind of *pattu* which is made up into tailored clothes. Finally, *chadars* may be turned over to the *gabba* makers to end their useful life as floor coverings.

Section of *chadar* from Bandipur, Kashmir

The rough homespun texture of the hand-woven village shawl and the intermix of primary colours in the *kani* weave to form a decorative border are the hallmarks of the peasant *chadar* or *loi*.

today the same basic type of loom is more often set up on a framework at floor level, with a bench for the weaver. It has four, foot-operated healds to make possible the twill weave, in which all the village fabrics are made. The shuttle is entirely different from that on a modern loom. It is a hollow cylinder into which the weft-yarn is stuffed after being manually wound round a long stick. This process is performed in such a manner that the yarn unravels smoothly, without tangles or further twisting as the shuttle travels. These traditional looms work on the throw-and-catch principle, which limits the width of the cloth to about 27 inches. *Chadars* are made up of two such widths stitched together.

In Kashmir proper and Ladakh, warping is done by means of pegs stuck in the ground; only in Gurez is a pegboard attached to a convenient wall used. The reason is that in this remote high-altitude valley, the short summer has to be exclusively devoted to work in the fields, and the entire weaving process must, therefore, be done indoors during the six snow-bound winter months. Standard practice all over the region is for warp yarn to be doubled and twisted and weft yarn only doubled. In most areas, the sheep are shorn twice a year, and the wool from the autumn clip — having a longer fibre-length — is reserved exclusively for the warp, while the less durable and shorter-fibred spring-sheared wool is used for the weft.

While the local *pattu* was woven in all the hill regions of the state in a great variety of weights and qualities, the most famous was that produced in Sopore. This variety apparently commanded more in the local market, since it was said to be in demand for military uniforms during the Second World War. The special quality of this *pattu* was its compact weave and the fine quality of the local yarns, mostly in natural colours, though vegetable dyes like walnut bark were occasionally used. It was woven in twill, typically in 60 cms widths. In addition to the ordinary *pattu*, there was a superfine quality in a plain weave called *kalami pattu*, the surface of which was so smooth that it was claimed possible to write on it with a pen. This was fine enough to make turbans for the richer farmers, and was also used for leggings. Sopore *pattu* was produced mainly by the somewhat depressed communities of Hajams, Wanis and Shalas. Unfortunately, the skills involved appear to have died out because of the easier profits obtained from apple cultivation.

Man spinning, Mulbekh, Ladakh

In Ladakh, spinning is done, not on the wheel, but on a hand-spindle or *tikli* which is about 24 cms long and as thick as a child's finger. As with the spinning-wheel, the raw wool is drawn out with the left hand while the right manipulates the *tikli*, no more than a length of wood worn smooth with years of use. The yarn for the Ladakhi *pattu*, *fruk pattu*, is spun exclusively by women, and is a perennial occupation, taken up when walking, chatting or selling vegetables, whenever hands are otherwise idle. In thicker spindles men produce a coarse yarn for agricultural accessories like sacks and ropes.

The other main product of the village looms, the *chadars*, display a wide variety of designs according to the areas in which they are woven. In Gurez, for instance, there are three distinct types. A common feature, however, is that none of the wool is dyed and the different designs are achieved by a judicious selection of various natural shades. Some are plain and unpatterned; then there is the *rawa* design — big, black-and-white multiple checks; and, thirdly, the charmingly-named *chashm-bulbul* — small, fine checks. Not all the Gurez fabrics are woven in sufficient widths for a *chadar* to be made up of only two; sometimes three have to be stitched together. Strangely enough, in a single village, in Tillel, an even remoter side-valley of Gurez, *rawa*-type *chadars* are made using yarn coloured with local vegetable dyes. These *chadars* are easy to confuse with the very similar ones woven in Kishtwar, though the same style probably evolved independently in the two widely separated areas.

The attractive bold designs of the Kishtwar and some of the Gurez *chadars* make it unnecessary for them to have contrast selvedge or borders. In this way they differ from the village *chadars* of the Kashmir valley, which are known as *kandidar*, bordered, in reference to their most distinctive feature. The finest *kandidar chadars* are said to come from the Bandipur area, where the *mohallas* of Nadihal, Kazipora and Papchal were famous for them, and where the weavers mainly belonged to the Shah, Syed and Pir communities.

Today, their manufacture is being encouraged by the state government's Handloom Development Project in Bandipur, but with certain modifications of the traditional methods. Mill-spun yarn is now supplied to the weavers who are also given fly-shuttle looms. This makes it possible for them to weave in 134 cms widths and to produce a *chadar* in two or three days, as opposed to the seven to ten days it takes on the old throw-and-catch looms. Villages almost equally famous for their *chadars* are Handwara, Magam, Tarzoo and Sopore.

Bandipur is only one of several areas to have been chosen by the Handloom Development Corporation for similar projects which aim at widening the range of traditional skills to encompass fabrics with definite market potential. Such fabrics now being produced in selected villages include *dosooti*, a heavy cotton destined to be embroidered with kashmir's famous crewel work, and *raffal*, a fine

Detail of *chhali*, Kargil, Ladakh

Goats' wool, locally spun, is woven into strips of 20 cms. widths and joined together with hand stitching to produce the *chhali* or *pherba*. Interspersing different shades of natural coloured wool, floor coverings, blankets and grain storage bags are made in homes for personal use. *Chhali* is the name widely used in the Suru valley of Kargil while the *pherba* and *tsokthal* define similar rough weaves in Leh district.

Far right
Village weaver at work, Mulbekh, Ladakh

The special feature of the Ladakhi loom is that it can be dismantled and reassembled within minutes, enabling the worker to set it up in sun or shade, according to the season. Like portable looms in other mountainous regions, from the Himalayas to the Andes, the Ladakhi one is narrow and the usual width of the *pattu* woven on it is about 35.6 cms. The manufacture of one such piece, 18 metres long, will occupy a weaver for one day in summer or two in winter.

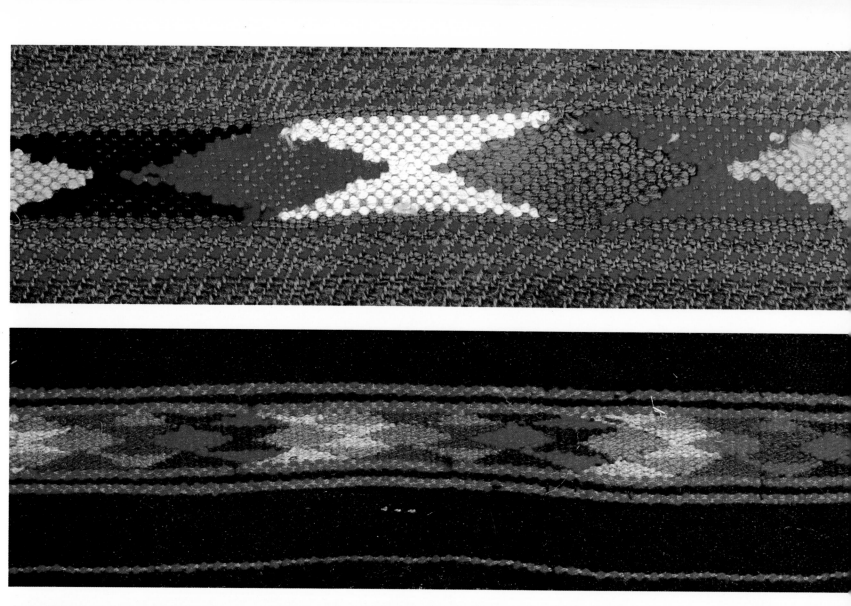

worsted mainly used for shawls. Pride of place in the officially-sponsored programme of handloom development goes to the production of export-quality tweeds, using local wool which is procured by the Corporation and prepared under commercial conditions. A wide range of designs has been developed, suitable for production on the fairly simple looms in use — plain weaves and hopsacks, twills and herringbones, plain and houndstooth checks — many of which pose an attractive challenge to an accomplished weaver and offer him the chance to extend his skills.

While this is clearly an "appropriate" mode of rural development, and the villages where it has been introduced show every sign of prosperity, it nevertheless involves a fundamental change in the nature of the work. The use of the fly-shuttle loom whose invention was one of the seminal events of the Industrial Revolution; the fact that the weaver, supplied with ready processed raw material, is responsible for only one phase of production and has no concern with the finishing of the cloth, which is destined for a distant market, not local use, suggests an emphasis on productivity at the expense of the craft aspect. Whatever the social and economic value of this kind of development, it cannot but have the effect of transforming a village craft into a cottage industry. It may be that the survival of the altogether exceptional spinning and weaving skills of Kashmir now lies not in the villages but solely in the pashmina industry.

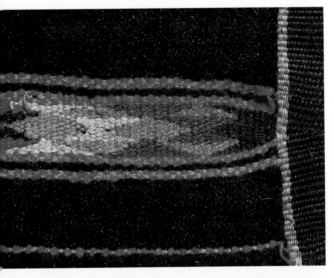

The availability of these skills, existing from time immemorial, provided the foundation for the development of the Kashmir shawl as a textile of unique softness, warmth and beauty. The other *sine qua non* was the finer than sheep's wool raw material which came in the form of the soft, delicate goat's fleece known the world over as "cashmere", but more properly referred to as *pashm*.

This luxurious fibre grows under the coarse and shaggy outer coat of a particular breed of the domestic goat, *Capra hircus*. Today, "cashmere" is the latest thing among livestock farmers in Australia and Scotland but in the past, its production was confined to the windswept, high-altitude pastures of Central Asia. The most extensive of these pastures were situated in the Chang-Thang plateau of western Tibet and contiguous south-eastern Ladakh. Today, the Chinese occupation of Tibet has slammed the door on supplies from the other

Kandidar bordered chadars of the Kashmir valley

Today, the contrast selvedges and borders are woven in commercially produced viscose; previously perhaps in silk, or even pashmina. While the selvedge is usually green or red, the end-border, *zanjeer*, about 1.3 cms to 2.5 cms in width, is in bright red, green, blue, white and yellow shades. These are composed into simple geometrical patterns, and each weaver has his particular design which constitutes his trademark. These *zanjeers* are woven by *kani* in a simpler form of the infinitely laborious and painstaking technique which went into the finest pashmina shawls of the 18th and 19th centuries. Whereas, those involve double interlocking at the colour junctions, the village weavers use the simpler "slit tapestry" technique without interlock; the designs are accordingly composed exclusively in diagonals, to avoid splitting.

side of the border; but the bulk of the *pashm* produced in Ladakh goes direct to Srinagar to fill the looms of the shawl weavers.

While *pashm* has been the basis of a multi-million rupee industry for centuries and occasionally a factor in high politics, another raw material for shawls, found in much smaller quantities, surpasses pashmina in softness and fineness to perhaps the same extent as pashmina surpasses ordinary sheep's wool. This is *tus*, the fleece that, like *pashm*, grows on certain goat-like wild animals whose habitat is similar, if not more extreme, than that of the pashmina goat. The two main sources of *tus* appear to be the ibex (*Capra ibex sibirica*), and the *chiru*, or Tibetan antelope (*Pantholope hodgsoni*). The Ladakhis, who ought to know, give pride of place to the *chiru*, a delicate deer-like animal whose two, long straight horns seen in profile, can give the illusion of a single horn. (It is pleasant to think of the legendary material *tus* being obtained from that even more legendary animal, the unicorn.) The Chang-pa – the nomadic herds-people who rear pashmina goats – trap and kill the *chiru* for its meat as well as its *tus* and also collect the *tus* that is shed naturally with the onset of summer and remains caught on rocks and bushes.

It is in working with these fine delicate materials that the skill of the Kashmiri spinners reaches its peak. In certain families of Srinagar and nearby villages it has been passed down from mother to daughter for generations beyond the counting of most of those engaged in it today. This kind of work is ideal for housebound women, for it is carried on in their own homes, and in whatever time they can spare from their domestic duties. It may be short on creativity, but the transformation of a mass of unattractive, matted wool — full of dust and other impurities, slightly greasy and mixed with the coarse outer hairs of the goat — into hanks of fine, soft and delicate yarn, must be a matter of recurrent satisfaction; and the manual skills involved are clearly of a very high order.

Today, the processing of raw *pashm* into yarn ready for the loom is done almost exactly according to the stages William Moorcroft described in detail in 1823 when, he tells us, 100,000 women were employed in it. As then, the raw *pashm* is bought from the wholesaler (who today may be the Government Wool Board); and the first task is to rid it of the coarse hair. This is done by hand, each small tuft of the *pashm* being teased out and the

hairs removed one by one. In the process, naturally a great deal of dust also comes out. The tedious and painstaking nature of this essential preliminary chore may be judged by the fact that it takes up to eight hours to de-hair 50 grams of *pashm*.

To rid the *pashm* of its slight natural oiliness, it is then thoroughly mixed with flour made from soaked and ground rice. This is applied damp and rubbed in well, and the *pashm* is then teased out once more, tuft by tuft, on a small wooden comb set vertically on a stand. This naturally disposes of most of the rice-flour and much of the remaining dust, while particularly tenacious particles are gently blown away or removed by the fingers.

After being spun, the yarn is doubled and twisted on the *yender* and with the aid of the *pritz*, a large reel, it is then wound into hanks. On resale back to the wholesaler from whom the raw fibre was bought, the 50 grams which cost the worker Rs.15-20, depending on its quality, will now fetch her anything from Rs.100-150 (1986 prices). Naturally, in a household which has several girls and women, all are likely to have participated in the several processes involved and the actual time taken to deal with 50 grams of *pashm* is around 20-25 woman-hours.

In the past, the weaving of pashmina shawls was done in the most intricate designs; but today most pashmina is woven in a plain twill, ready to receive the embroidery which gives the nearest approximation to the old-style "cashmere" shawls, or else in stripes and checks.

While plain pashmina weaving is completely different from *kani* weaving, despite the fact that they use identical looms, it also bears very little resemblance to modern handloom weaving on the fly-shuttle loom. For a start, the delicacy of the yarns means that they are liable to break, and the regularity of the throw-and-catch motions is continually interrupted to deal with this. Secondly, the monotonous clack-clack of the fly-shuttle is eliminated. A pashmina weaver's workshop — in which five or six looms may be packed into a space the size of a small bedroom — presents a picture of quiet concentration and unhurried movement, the only sound, beyond a little desultory conversation, being the bubbling of the master-weaver's *hukka*, the intermittent whirring of the *yender* as weft threads are wound from the *pritz* or reel to the straw bobbins ready to be loaded into the shuttles, and the muted

Top and bottom

Chadar from Kishtwar

The village *chadars* of the Kashmir valley and its neighbouring mountains have evolved a number of distinct and characteristic styles in the various districts. Those of Kishtwar are patterned in bold checks, which use wool coloured by local vegetable and mineral dyes as well as exploiting the different natural shades.

and the muted thud of the comb on the fell of the cloth. If *tus* is being woven on any of the looms the motion is even gentler, and the impact of the comb on the fell is softer.

The peculiar feature of the famous Kashmir shawls of the 18th and 19th centuries is that the design, like tapestry, was woven into the very fabric of the cloth. This was done by replacing the shuttle used in ordinary weaving with a series of small, eyeless wooden bobbins known in Kashmiri as *kani*, each filled with coloured yarn. The work was done by two or three weavers seated at one loom. The "wrong" side of the material was uppermost and the weavers interlaced the *kanis* through the warp-ends according to the instructions of the master-weaver or *ustad* who read aloud from a shorthand pattern called *talim*. Blindly following the instructions — "lift three and use red; lift eight and use green; lift five and use yellow" they progressed by infinitesimal stages across the width of the loom, often completing in a day no more picks of the weft than it took to make a quarter-inch of the pattern.

In the old days, the *kani* weavers were known as *khandwao*, a word of characteristic Kashmiri subtlety which sums up all that the weaver was — one who worked with infinite dexterity but blindly, without any conception of the larger design emerging under his skilled fingers. Indeed, it would be strange if he had, or was even interested in having, any such conception. For in the 18th and 19th centuries, the weavers whose skills made the name of Kashmir famous throughout the civilised world as the origin of shawls — whose excellence others could emulate but never hope to equal — were the most miserable and depressed class of the population. From the time of the Mughals, successive governments in Kashmir — the Afghans, the Sikhs and the Dogras — identified the shawl industry as a fruitful source of revenue and used every expedient to squeeze the last possible paisa from it. This went to the extent of deducting a portion from the weaver's meagre wage to pay for government-supplied rice at a rate higher than that prevailing in the open market.

The squeeze continued all the way down, through a network of government inspectors, merchants, middlemen, brokers, workshop owners, *karkhanadars, ustads* and superior workers like pattern-drawers, *naqash;* pattern-colourers, *tarah-guru;* and pattern-writers, *talim-guru* — each level en-

suring that they should not be the losers. The entire weight of the pyramid finally came to rest on the back of the wretched *khandwao*, who formed its base and had no one beneath him to pass it on to. The emigration of weavers was forbidden and the passes watched but some escaped to set up weaving communities in the Punjab. Weavers were no better than bonded serfs, forbidden to change their calling, or even to move from one workshop to another. And there are pathetic tales of workers cutting off their thumbs rather than enduring such back-breaking and thankless toil any longer. The weaver's work involved bending over his loom from dawn to dusk, in rooms which — if contemporary accounts are to be believed — were usually ill-lit, unventilated and without any heating in winter. The weaver was, therefore, instantly recognisable in a crowd because of his feeble and sickly physique. And if there was any doubt, a glance at his delicate hands — utterly unsuited to guide the plough — confirmed the identification. Indeed, if ever an article of beauty and worth was fashioned in the blood, sweat, toil and tears of the exploited worker, that was the *kani* shawl of Kashmir.

The origin of the *kani* pashmina is lost in the mist of time, legend and tradition. The *kani* technique is not, in fact, peculiar to Kashmir and was used in the traditional weaves of different tribes of Central Asia and Persia for the *kilims*, saddle-bags and blankets of everyday use. Although the neolithic artefacts found at the Burzahom archaeological site include flint and bone objects in the exact shape and size of *kanis*, we cannot be certain that they were actually used or whether the technique originated in Kashmir or further to the north and west. Kashmir, however, was the only area where it came to be combined with a twill weave to make the sophisticated products of the urban civilisation on a commercial scale.

While scattered passages in Sanskrit literature from a very early date may be interpreted as references to the raw material, *pashm*, or the technique, *kani*, or both, they are not sufficiently definite to warrant the firm conclusion that *kani* pashmina existed in ancient and medieval India. The most suggestive reference before the Mughal period is in the *Rajatarangini* of Srivara, the late 15th century Kashmiri text which mentions manufacture of fine woollen cloth with woven patterns which "filled even painters with surprise". Local tradition associates

Woman spinning *pashm* in her home, Srinagar

The Kashmiri spinning-wheel or *yender* consists of either a pair of wooden discs set parallel to each other at a distance of about 5 cms, their edges widely notched; or of two wheels whose thick, carved spokes extend a few centimetres beyond the circle which joins them. Either way, by use of the notches or the protruding spokes, a thick cord is wound along and between the two circles, forming a yielding and discontinuous rim. It is turned by means of a handle, and another cord passing over the rim transfers the movement from the wheel to the spindle. A length of paddy-straw is slipped over the spindle to serve as a bobbin, on to which the spun yarn is wound. When full, it can be slipped off and replaced.

The same spinning-wheel is used in the villages of Kashmir to spin sheep's wool for *pattus* and *chadars*, and in the *mohallas* of Srinagar by the women who spin the much finer fibres of *pashm*, used for the softest shawls.

Women processing raw *pashm*. Srinagar

The comb is used to prepare the cleaned fibres for spinning. The peculiar design of the spinning-wheel or *yender* is explained by Moorcroft as conducive to "a continuance of soft elastic movements without jerk or stiffness, to prevent the yarn breaking on the occurrence of any slight interruption in drawing it out". The woman on the left is winding the doubled yarn into hanks from the *pritz*, a large reel with a handle, using the simple means of two large nails set 18 cms apart in a wooden plank. The hanks will be divided into 20-thread bundles tied with coloured cotton.

the origins of shawl manufacture with the great figures of Kashmir's medieval history, Syed Ali Handani and Sultan Zain-ul-Abadin; and the introduction of *pashm* with the Central Asian conquerer, Mirza Haidar Daughlat, in the early 16th century.

The first circumstantial accounts come from the Mughal period. The *Ain-i-Akbari* indicates clearly enough that by the late 16th century the Kashmir shawl industry was an old and well-established one. "In former times shawls were often brought from Kashmir... His Majesty encourages, in every possible way, the manufacture of shawls in Kashmir." In his memoirs, the Mughal emperor Jehangir remarks that the shawls of Kashmir "are very famous; there is no need to praise them". Francois Bernier's description in the mid-17th century leaves no room for doubt that he is referring to the same *kani* pashmina shawls that were to become famous as Kashmir (or "cashmere") shawls. They are made, he says, both of sheep's wool, and of goat's wool from Tibet, "ornamented at both ends with a kind of embroidery made on the loom, a foot in width."

The earliest extant samples of *kani* pashmina date from probably the first half of the 17th century , and reveal a sophistication of design and technique that indicate a long-established and highly developed craft. Evidence for the type of design that was in vogue comes from these and other pieces of the Mughal period (which in terms of Kashmir's history means up to 1753, when Mughal rule gave way to Afghan rule), together with some contemporary paintings. Shawls have a large plain centre field, with narrow borders along the two sides. The main feature of the design is the deep end-borders, the most usual theme of which is the single repeated flower, rendered in a highly naturalistic manner and occupying enough space to show it off to the best advantage. In their lightness and delicacy, these floral motifs are reminiscent of other expressions of Mughal art, like the flower-paintings in royal albums, or the inlay work on the walls of the Taj Mahal. The narrow borders along the selvedges and those enclosing the main design of the end-borders, are often composed of a meandering-flower pattern which may echo an element in the main motif.

Although the development of design is a continuous process, earlier forms are not necessarily superseded, but may continue to exist alongside the new concepts. Thus, the analysis of such de-velopment can, at best, be tentative. Even so, it is sometimes possible to discern major shifts, and one such occurs in *kani* design from about the middle of the 18th century, with the abandoning of the characteristic restraint of the Mughal style and the beginnings of a trend towards even greater elaboration. The floral motif now begins a process of evolution that transforms it from a single bloom into an increasingly stylised bunch or bouquet, and eventually into the famous "cone" shape in its many and varied forms.

The tear-drop or cone motif, however, was not a new one and is found as early as the Babylonian civilisation, where it is believed to have represented the growing shoot of the all-nourishing date palm, and hence to have stood as a symbol of the Tree of Life — one of the oldest and most powerful of all archetypes. It figures in early Coptic, Egyptian and Byzantine art and was an important element in medieval Persian design. Therefore, it was probably a motif well-known to the Kashmiri shawl designers, who seized on it as the form best suited to express an aesthetic sense now liberated from the restraints of the more austere Mughal canon. Simultaneously, with its appearance in *kani* design, it is also found for the first time in other expressions of the Kashmiri creative genius — such as manuscript illumination, papier maché and metal-work. Some analyses also suggest that in adopting this form the Kashmiri imagination was enriched by such purely local inspirations as the meandering course of the river Jhelum near Srinagar, or even the eddying of the current around the foundations of the city's seven bridges.

In the early 19th century there was much more to *kani* pashmina than merely shawls. Moorcroft's list of the "shawl-goods" being produced in 1823 includes no fewer than 94 items, most of them grouped in four major categories. These are: *do-shala* or shawls in pairs, typically 3¾ *gaz* × 1½ *gaz* (3.21 m × 1.27 m); *qasaba* or *rumal*, square shawls for women's wear, 1½ to 2½ *gaz* square (1.27 m to 2.12 m); *jamawar* or gown-pieces, in the same measurements as *do-shala*; and; *shamla* or waist-girdles, 8 *gaz* × 1½ *gaz* (6.77 m × 1.27 m). Miscellaneous items included *lungis* or checked girdles, stockings and socks, leggings, trousers, floor-coverings, curtains, saddle-cloths for horses and elephants, purses, and canopies for tombs.

It seems worthwhile to consider the word *jamawar*.

Far left

Kanihama pashmina weaving by *kanis*

Kanis are small, eyeless bobbins used instead of the shuttle. Each *kani* is filled with coloured yarn and is used to weave the colours into the warp in sequence, according to the pattern. In the 19th century, the number of *kanis* across the width of the loom is said to have varied between 400 and an incredible 1,500, according to the intricacy of the design. In the less complex work done today, the usual number is around 80-100. The solidity of the weft-faced fabric, with no break at the colour junctions, is achieved by the technique of interlocking the thread from each *kani* with the one used before and after.

Centre

Kanihama pashmina weaver at work using *kanis*

The loom on which pashmina is woven in Kashmir is the same, whether the work is plain or patterned. It is a compact affair taking up little space, barely 85 cms, from the warp-beam to the weaver's back-rest. The warp-beam, healds and comb are suspended from the ceiling, the former is attached by a peg and cord to a fixed beam beneath it and this arrangement enables it to be turned as required to let off the warp. The cloth-beam is also tightened manually. The healds are operated in the usual way by treadles; and for both the *kanis* required for patterning and the slim small shuttle used for plain work, only a narrow shed is required.

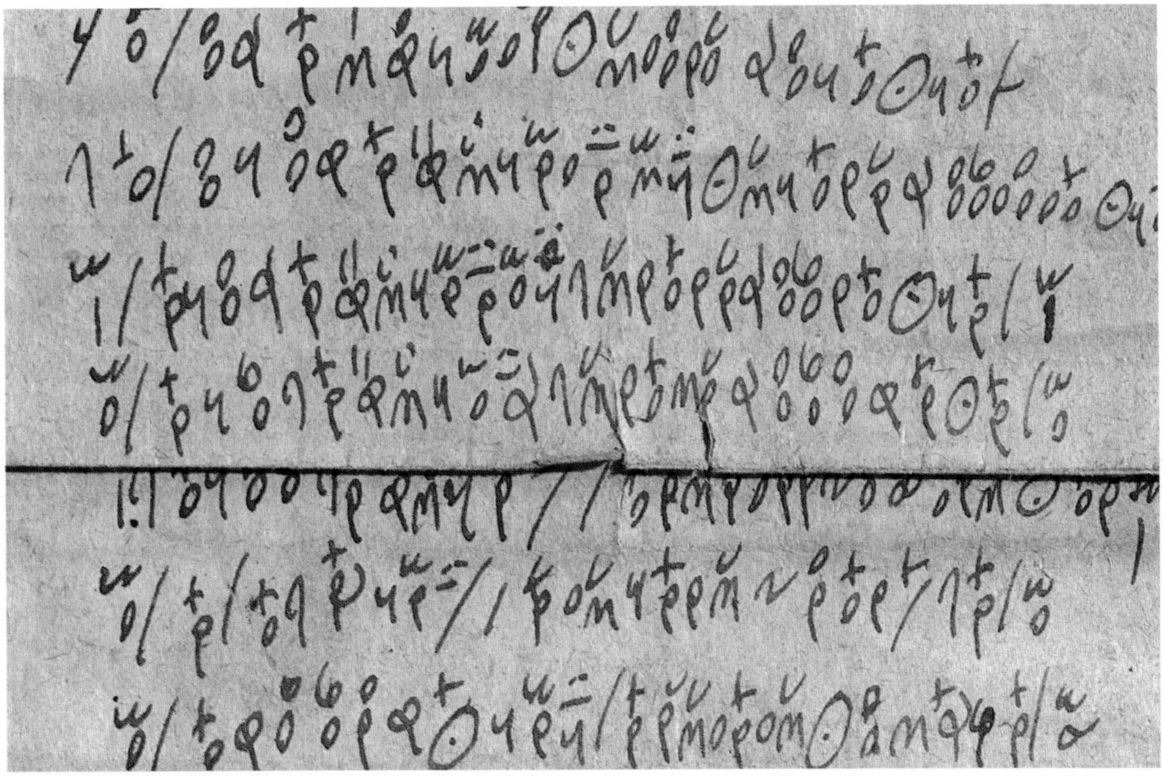

Talim for *cheet misri* shawl; 1830; Kanihama, Kashmir

A *talim* prepared around 1830 for the *cheet misri kani* design, an all-over floral pattern. The code indicates the number of threads of the same colour to be used in a line of weaving. The master weaver reads aloud while the weavers follow his directions carefully. Each figure in the code stands for a colour.

Ǒ = green (*zargari*)
Ö = white (*chot*)
Ô = pink (*gulabi*)
Q̱ = yellow (*zard*)
Ȯ̱ = pomegranate (*anari*)

and so on.

The invention of the *talim* made it possible to codify *kani* patterns in a very small space. When the Europeans began to imitate the Kashmir shawl and wanted to record designs, the best way they could manage to do so was by means of graph paper, each square representing the intersection of one thread of the warp with one of the weft. Such patterns were, naturally, many times bigger than the shawls they represented.

the first time, primarily an article of women's rather than men's attire. But it was not till the Napoleonic period that it became a garment of high fashion, the style being set by the Empress Josephine after she had received, it is said, a gift of two pieces from Napoleon to whom they had been presented by the Khedive of Egypt. For the next 60 years, the shawl was an indispensable adjunct to the wardrobe of every fashionable woman in Europe, particularly in France. And this was the period of the greatest productivity of the industry in Kashmir, as well as of the greatest change and development in design.

During the last 20 years of Afghan rule and the 27 years of Sikh domination, which covered the first half of the 19th century, the trend towards greater elaboration continued. While the cone remained the most important element in the design of the shawls intended for export to India, Persia, Russia and western Europe, there was an immense variety of other designs, especially in *jamawar*. An important one of these was *khatirast*, stripes, which were made up of indefinite motifs, or of the meandering-flower designs used for narrow borders. Among both *do-shala* and *rumal* a popular design was the *chand-dar*, with a large circle or "moon" in the centre, made up of floral or other motifs on a plain or patterned ground, and often four quarter-moons in the corners.

It is not always possible to correlate the terms used in Moorcroft's list with those mentioned by experts in Kashmir today. Some of the latter, which must have evolved during the Afghan period, are identified as *punjdar*, a five-petalled flower; *poshkar*, or bouquet; *badamgar*, or almond, one of the many forms of the cone; *kyuposh*, another floral motif; and *gul-e-anar*, pomegranate blossom. An all-over flower pattern is known as *cheet-misri*, indicating that it was particularly popular in the Egyptian market. The *shah-pasand* or "royal choice" seems invariably to be made up of cones.

During the later Afghan period, dozens of variants of the basic cone made their appearance. Now it was a vase of flowers, now a bouquet, now a cypress, now an almond, now one of many purely conventional shapes framing a complex floral pattern. After Afghan rule gave way to Sikh rule, a further tendency was for the cones to increase in size, and for the design — originally confined to the end and side-border — to invade the centre field. The early part of the Dogra period, which started in 1846,

marked the culmination of these developments.

By now, the export of shawls to Europe had become a very big business. And, as with the Asian markets established in the 18th century, the European — mainly French — market created a demand for particular types of designs. French shawl companies actually sent designs to Kashmir to be executed there. Moreover, the Jacquard loom, Europe's answer to the infinitely laborious and time-consuming *kani* technique, on which an increasing number of shawls was now being woven in Europe itself, was favourable to a particular kind of sweeping all-over pattern, which became a major influence on the Kashmir shawl in its last years. This led to major shifts in design and a move away from traditional canons, which may have been one of the factors responsible for the rapid decline and collapse of the industry which practically disappeared by the end of the century.

During the third quarter of the 19th century, there arose a combination of several circumstances which together wrote the death-warrant of an industry that had given a livelihood to thousands. Conventional wisdom puts the beginning of the end to 1870, with the Franco-Prussian war and France's subsequent defeat, which caused such psychological and material trauma that the luxuriousness associated with the shawl fashion died out. It is no doubt true, as reported by Lawrence, that the weaving community followed the course of the war with intense interest, "bursting into tears and loud lamentations when the news of Germany's victories reached them". But there were other factors tending in the same direction.

Shawl weavers who had escaped from the inhuman conditions of work in Kashmir had established weaving communities in the Punjab, from where goods made of inferior wools, but passed off as the genuine Kashmir article, flooded the European market. And by the end of the century the use of more complex looms — the draw-loom, the harness-loom and finally the Jacquard loom — had enabled the European centres of shawl-manufacture like Paris, Lyons, Vienna, Norwich and most of all Paisley, to produce shawls which, in terms of design and regularity of work (though not of technique and raw material) were the equal of anything that Kashmir could show, and at a fraction of the price of the real thing. This brought the shawl-fashion within the reach of the lower and

Fragment of *kani* material, *cheet misri* design; 1830; Kanihama, Kashmir

Cheet misri was made up largely into *kasabas* or square shawls for women's wear, presumably for the Egyptian market. On the basis of an all-over floral pattern, different pieces seem to vary according to the styles of different periods. While some from the early mid-18th century have all the grace and delicacy of Mughal design, this example reflects the over-elaboration characteristic of the Sikh period.

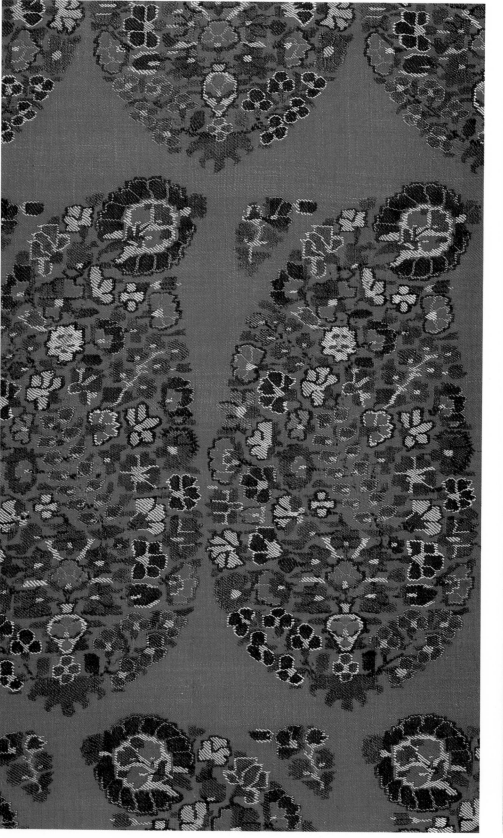
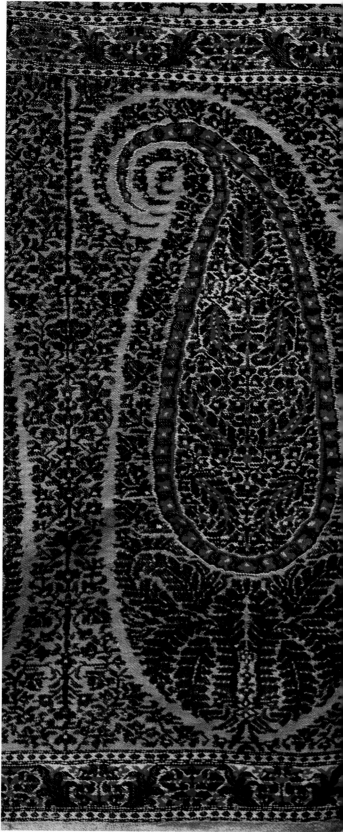

Far left

Detail of *kani* shawl; perhaps late 18th century; School of Designs, Srinagar

While the characteristic motif of shawl design in the Mughal period appears to have been the single flower, conceived and executed with the utmost delicacy, the replacement of Mughal by Afghan rule sees the beginning of a trend towards ever-greater elaboration. As the purity and restraint of the Mughal style are gradually abandoned, the single botanically identifiable flower is largely replaced by a bunch of increasingly stylised flower-forms, often presented rising from a vase or dish. It would seem to be the curved lines of this that gradually, over the years of Afghan rule and during the early part of the Sikh period (1819-46), crystallised into the cone shape (also described as mango, almond, cypress, tear-drop and paisley) which in its various forms came to dominate shawl design right to the end.

Centre

Detail of *kani* shawl; mid-19th century; School of Designs, Srinagar

During the later Sikh and the Dogra periods, the cone undergoes a process of variation and metamorphosis which takes it even farther from its origin as a bunch or vase of flowers than the latter was from the Mughal-style single bloom. This example shows an elegant, but highly stylised scroll-like form, with little or no relationship to any floral motif, its elongated extremities almost merging with the elaborate background.

Detail of *shah-pasand* shawl; second half of 19th century; Sri Pratap Singh Museum, Srinagar

The basic cone-shape which evolved in the later 18th century has now become heavy and lost much of its earlier grace. The most striking feature of the design, however, is the filling in of the originally plain background, the cone itself standing out only by virtue of its narrow outline. Throughout the Sikh period *kani* designs developed an ever-increasing complexity, with the introduction of architectural motifs and others equally inimical to the purity of the earlier Mughal style.

dustry that had given a livelihood to thousands. Conventional wisdom puts the beginning of the end to 1870, with the Franco-Prussian war and France's subsequent defeat, which caused such psychological and material trauma that the luxuriousness associated with the shawl fashion died out. It is no doubt true, as reported by Lawrence, that the weaving community followed the course of the war with intense interest, "bursting into tears and loud lamentations when the news of Germany's victories reached them". But there were other factors tending in the same direction.

Shawl weavers who had escaped from the inhuman conditions of work in Kashmir had established weaving communities in the Punjab, from where goods made of inferior wools, but passed off as the genuine Kashmir article, flooded the European market. And by the end of the century the use of more complex looms — the draw-loom, the harness-loom and finally the Jacquard loom — had enabled the European centres of shawl-manufacture like Paris, Lyons, Vienna, Norwich and most of all Paisley, to produce shawls which, in terms of design and regularity of work (though not of technique and raw material) were the equal of anything that Kashmir could show, and at a fraction of the price of the real thing. This brought the shawl-fashion within the reach of the lower and middle classes, and by that very token reduced the demand for the expensive genuine article among the rich and fashionable. A simultaneous development was the change in style of women's dress. Both the straight lines of the "Empire" look at the beginning of the century, and the curves of the mid-century crinoline were well complemented by the trailing drapery of the shawl; but not so the bustle which came into fashion in the late 1860s, and which demanded a more severe and tailored look.

While these external factors combined to reduce the demand for shawls abroad, in Kashmir a disastrous famine in 1877-78 decimated the weak and sickly weaving community. It would have taken a better organised industry, and one which received positive encouragement from the authorities instead of being regarded as no more than a source of revenue, to have withstood this series of misfortunes.

In the 1860s — the final flowering of the industry — there are said to have been 800 *karkhanadars* in the valley, implying perhaps eight to ten times that number of looms and about 25,000 weavers; by 1901 there were no more than 5,000 weavers, declining to a mere 148 in 1911. The shawl-industry's loss was the carpet-industry's gain and many former *kani* weavers are reported to have taken to carpet-work, which happened to enjoy a revival from the mid-1870s. The carpet-industry also took over many of the *kani* designs and the *talim* system.

A continuing, though reduced, demand from India, and also initially from Persia, kept the shawl industry going through the first half of the present century; and this has, no doubt, increased since Independence with the prosperity following economic development. The growth of Kashmir as a tourist destination must also have stimulated demand. But the events of the later 19th century dealt the death-blow to the extraordinary skills of the *kani* weavers, and the finest shawls of this century are of plain pashmina decorated with the delicate embroidery for which Kashmir is so famous.

Although the *kani* weaving techniques have not been lost altogether, the almost unbelievable skill associated with the great days of the industry seems to have disappeared. The basic technique is kept alive — but only just — by a handful of families in Kanihama on the Gulmarg road, and two or three nearby villages. Today, they are supported by a government-sponsored project which is attempting a revival on a commercial basis. If such government intervention can be based unequivocally on the premise that the skill is worth preserving for its own sake, and that profitability must take second place, then there might possibly be some hope that the technique will not only survive, but enjoy a revival of something like its past glory.

Detail of *kani* shawl; probably 1860s; School of Designs, Srinagar

The Jacquard designs used by shawl manufacturers in Europe had a profound influence on *kani* design. Thus the cone entered the final phase of its development as an abstraction, a scroll, often less a unit on its own than part of an over-all complexity of pattern. It was these shawls, reinterpreting design concepts derived from an alien technique in a Kashmiri idiom, that were invariably composed of a patch-work of many pieces. While the result was often rich and luxurious the marriage of Jacquard designs with *kani* technique was often not aesthetically successful, and in the shawls of the industry's great period, the exuberance of the Sikh period design often degenerated into coarseness, even vulgarity. This general decline of artistic standards, however, did not preclude the production of particular exquisite pieces, and certainly implied no lowering of the standard of an infinitely painstaking craftsmanship. In 1853, a particularly gorgeous shawl on order for the Empress of France is said to have taken 30 men nine months' full-time work to complete.

Embroidery

The close link between nature, history and the crafts of Jammu and Kashmir is reflected in the characteristics and development of embroidery, particularly in the Kashmir valley. In this region, the embroidery draws inspiration from the gentle colours of the landscape, from the flowers and birds and from the elaborate designs evolved during the halcyon days of the famous *kani* shawl.

Walking down the congested by-lanes of Srinagar, one often comes across men sitting near the windows of their living rooms, fabric on their knees, empty thread baskets and rolls of thread spread out on the floor. There is silence in the room, except for the younger generation of craftsmen whispering to each other and passing thread through the needle, while the elders intently follow the needle as it adds another colourful line to the fabric. This is a common sight in the valley of Kashmir and is different from other parts of the country where embroidery is done by women and the motivation is not entirely commercial.

In Kashmir, the origin of embroidery is closely linked to court patronage and subsequent market de-

mand, once it achieved a certain excellence in design, weaving technique, stitch work and aesthetic appeal. Thus, unlike other parts of India, embroidered shawls, bedspreads or wall-hangings were not for the daughter's trousseau nor did they have a functional use in the craftsman's simple dwelling. Embroidery was not a medium for carrying forward local folk traditions. The attitude to work and the changes which have taken place in the past five centuries have been mainly a result of the craftsman's need to survive and cater to markets in the country and abroad. Around the 14th century, embroidery responded to the demand from Central Asian bazaars, then to the European market and finally to the growing need in India itself.

Embroidery work in Kashmir, except for *zari* embroidery where women outnumber men, is the prerogative of males. This is probably due to the influence of the Sayyids, Sufi dervishes from the neighbouring Muslim areas. With their overpowering influence and piety, the Sayyids strove hard to establish an Islamic way of life, of which the seclusion of women was very much a part.

A chain of craftsmen including the *naqash* or designer who is the printer, the *khandwao* or weaver, and the *raffoogar* or darner, produced the famed woven pashmina shawl on the *kani* loom and later the plain base for embroidered shawls.

It was Zain-ul-Abadin (1400-1470) who introduced the art of fine weaving in the valley and the patterns on woven shawls were subsequently copied by embroiderers. According to local legend, the embroidered shawl was a creation of a *raffoogar* called Alibaba, who lived in the time of the Afghan ruler Azad Khan. Alibaba, it is said, once noticed the imprints of a fowl's feet left on a white sheet and proceeded to embroider the outline with coloured thread, to beautiful effect. Legend apart, given the conditions of the weavers, the tax structure in the state and the demand for Kashmiri shawls in the European market, it was more likely the business ingenuity of an Armenian trader, Khwaja Yusuf, along with the deft hands of an Alibaba that led to the origin of the embroidered or *amli* shawl.

When Khwaja Yusuf came to Kashmir from Constantinople to purchase woven shawls, he found they were very expensive. The taxation on them and on the sale price made them even less attractive for markets abroad. That was probably when the idea of copying the patterns with a needle was born. And, since embroidered shawls were exempt from taxes and yet retained an aesthetic appeal, Alibaba, the *raffoogar*, was able to give shape to Khwaja Yusuf's business plans to reduce production costs.

This ingenious plan revived the shawl industry which was collapsing under the burden of heavy taxation and stiff competition from inexpensive, woven shawls produced in Lyons and Paisley. In the process, a new trend in the long history of Kashmir shawl-making was created.

There is no evidence which can help us trace the history of embroidery to its origin, for textiles are perishable and very few examples prior to the 17th century have survived. Eleventh century wall paintings found in monasteries in Ladakh provide proof of the fine work done by Kashmiri craftsmen. The exquisite, embroidered garments worn by the figures painted on the walls of the Alchi monastery indirectly establish the existence of a pattern on the surface and are by no stretch of imagination shawls.

During the Mughal period (1586-1752), while the *kani* technique was at its peak in Kashmir, embroidery was fairly advanced in the rest of India and court workshops were established in Delhi for craftsmen to embellish fabrics. In Kashmir, this tradition may have been overshadowed by the *kani* technique which resulted in some of the finest pieces of loom-woven shawls. The art of needlework in the state was, therefore, first limited to joining separately woven pieces, although it is possible that some shawls were embroidered in gold and silver thread. The decline of the Mughal empire after the end of Aurangzeb's reign, followed by political uncertainty in the valley, made way for the Afghan ruler Ahmad Shah Durrani in 1752 to conquer the valley.

The six decades of Afghan dominance were characterised by extreme hardship and poverty for the inhabitants of the valley. The shawl industry, whose output included *amli* shawls, was viewed as a source of revenue and the Afghans followed a policy of deriving maximum benefit, even at the cost of suppressing the craftsmen.

Around the same time the Sikhs were evolving in stature in the plains and had turned militant in their confrontation with the existing spiritual and poli-

Previous page

Present-day *karkhana* on the banks of the Jhelum river, Srinagar

Embroiderers work on chain stitch rugs and furnishing fabric in a room where their tools, raw materials, dyed thread and spindles can be seen. The work is supervised by a senior craftsman who sits on the balcony overlooking the river, suggesting changes and colours and keeping an account of the thread used in every rug made in the *karkhana*.

Silk patchwork *thankha*; mid-19th century; Ladakh

Thankhas are scrolls of religious art, usually handpainted. This is a rare patchwork *thankha* worked by an artist from Saboo village depicting Padma Sambhava, founder of the Red Sect of Buddhism and professor of Occult Science at Nalanda University. To counter the local animist religion of the Bön-pa, Padma Sambhava was called to visit Tibet to win over the people with his learning and spiritual powers. As the father of Lamaism he is believed to have studied in Kashmir and lived for some time in Ladakh.

This piece is said to be one of the six hand embroidered *thankhas* existing in Ladakh today.

tical powers. After establishing themselves as a military power in Lahore, the Sikhs slowly acquired strength to gain a foothold in the valley.

The coming of the Sikhs, who were famous for their love of brilliance and colour, infused an Indian element into textiles once again and after they established their hold over the state a distinct change in embroidery is evident. Sikh rule is believed to have been one of the most creative periods in the life cycle of the embroidered shawl. Earlier Islamic tradition had forbidden the use of figurative decorations and the emphasis had been on floral and geometric designs. Now, human figures and *shikar* scenes started appearing on fabrics. These shawls were known as *shikargah* and they captured and recorded moments of triumph in the forest in coloured silk.

At a later point, the French trading companies stationed in the state introduced designs generally acceptable in Europe where parallel styles were in vogue at the time. One style completely hid the colour of the fabric with work in minute stitches covering every inch of space with human figures, floral patterns and the overwhelming cones, which had by now elongated. The second style followed the pattern of square shawls with a medallion in the centre and quarter medallions in the four corners.

In Kashmir, since embroidery did not begin as a domestic craft, it was organised professionally in Srinagar under the technical guidance of master craftsmen from the start. By the late 18th century small manufacturing units employing weavers, pattern makers, dyers and embroiderers worked under one roof. Some of them took to marketing and opened sales outlets in the city and elsewhere in India. This system has not undergone a major change but, in order to streamline the process, dyeing, weaving and embroidery is given to a group of workers who work at home. Embroidery is carried out more diligently during the winter months when little work can be done in the fields.

Even today, when some of the work is carried out inside the home, the most experienced workman automatically takes the lead in giving directions and making modifications wherever necessary. The senior craftsman understands the needs of the client, discusses the colours, negotiates the deal and within this framework guides his team of

Old man embroiders a raffal **shawl on the outskirts of Srinagar**

In winter months the whole family, which includes a specialist, huddle in a warm room. Coarse embroidery work on shawls and rugs is mainly done in small towns and villages. Fine work on pashmina, formerly undertaken in establishments within the city limits, is now carried out by craftsmen who are farmers by profession and who spend a considerable time tilling the soil.

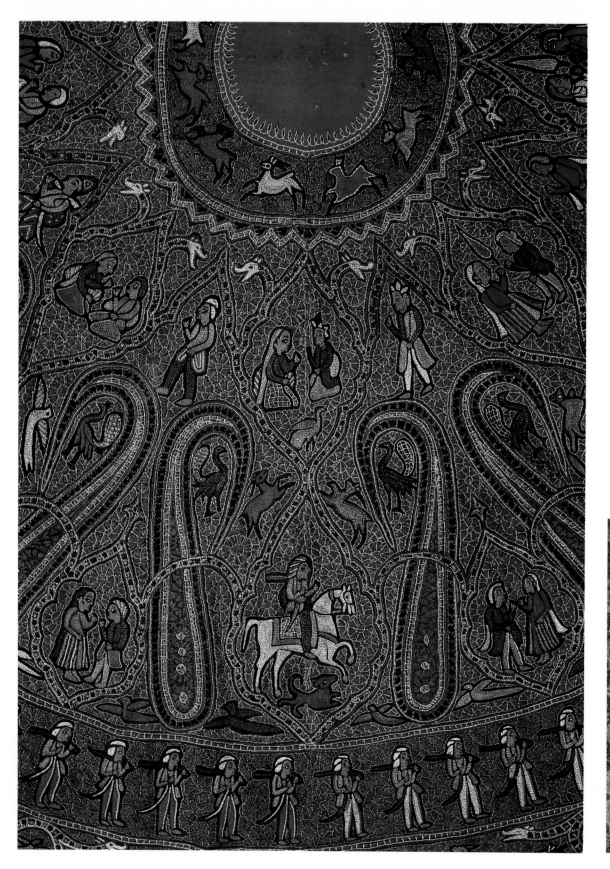

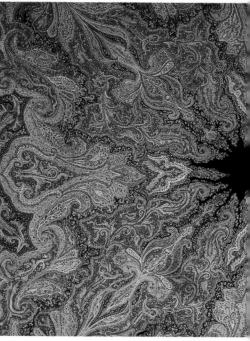

craftsmen in achieving the desired results. *Karkha-nas* exclusively devoted to embroidery have evolved since the beginning of the 20th century.

With the flowering of the shawl trade during the Mughal period, two main forms of production were established — the *tili* or *kanikar* which was the woven shawl, and the *amlikar* which was the embroidered one. In the former the design evolved on the loom itself, while the latter came about by the use of the needle. A catalogue of an exhibition of crafts held in India in 1903 states: "Except for the very most expensive loom shawls the needle is in-variably used to furnish certain portions of the de-sign in all the loom shawls". Patchwork loom shawls were equal lengths of ribbon sewn together, while patchwork embroidered shawls were com-posed of irregularly formed patches with separate pieces of cloth forming areas with different colour effects. Sometimes, pieces from two or three old shawls would be used to build up a new shawl with straight strips of *amli* work covering the remaining areas. These could be called restoration shawls and were constructed and joined entirely with the needle.

Watt and Percy in their catalogue deduce that "the degree of needlework detected on a loom shawl may be accepted as the extent of the weaver's admission of defective workmanship". At least in some cases, *amli* work should, therefore, be under-stood as that particular form of embroidery de-signed exclusively to imitate or supplement *kani* work.

Some of the designs in pashminas and *jamawars* may have been exclusively embroidered. The stitch, a kind of parallel darn, lifted the loop of the warp so cleverly that it was often almost impossible to differentiate between weaving and embroidery. The embroiderer caught in all the loose ends of the weave, highlighted the edges of patterns in silk threads of different colours and rendered the tex-ture free of imperfections. The highlighting of the edges was done in obliquely overlapping short darn stitch. The border pieces of woven and embroidered patterns were joined to the plain cen-tral field so neatly that it could not be distinguished. At times, the embroiderer often carried the design further on to the central area, thus strengthening and further disguising the join. Similarly, corner medallions and sprays were often needle-worked while the borders were woven. If the weave or the

Far left

Tablecloth in *sozani* or needlework; 19th century; Sri Pratap Singh Museum; Srinagar.

This tablecloth is embroidered with a large round medallion containing figures and anim-als around a central floral motif. The pictorial square is worked with a variety of animals, armed men on horseback and courting cou-ples. The embroidered peacocks may be sym-bolic of romance. The piece was probably in-spired by the miniature paintings of the neigh-bouring hill states. Scenes of gaiety, love and valour find a permanent record on similar *rumals* or embroidered squares.

***Amlikar* shawl; late 19th century; SPS Museum; Srinagar, Kashmir**

A central, black sun-burst medallion is sur-rounded by a stylised lobed medallion. The top of the medallion fits into the space be-tween two black rays of the sunburst medal-lion. The remaining portion has been filled with stylised vines whose leaves converge on the prominent black centre. The *jamawar* or *kani* is a combination of *kanikar* and *amlikar*. A majority of shawls were later a patchwork of loom-woven strips of pashmina finally sewn together in an elaborate pattern. The embroid-ery defines and refines the woven pattern.

embroidery was done to appear exactly the same on both sides it was known as *dorukha*, while a comparatively untidily finished under-portion categorised the shawl as *ekrukha*.

There has been so much intermingling and repetition of designs that it is not always possible to place them in compartments and say for certain that a particular pattern belonged to a specific period. The quality of work may vary but in general the patterns are repeated in different colours.

The most dominant motif in Kashmiri embroidery is the *boteh*, flower, which has persisted all along in different forms, evolving from a simple, freely-spaced floral arrangement to a sweeping and complex scroll by the middle of the 19th century. The highly-stylised patterns commonly done on shawls were a creation of aesthetically evolved minds over a period of three centuries. When they were implemented they gave rise to a new trend in the local courts from where they slowly permeated to other social levels.

The abundance of colours has made an impact on the minds of Kashmiri craftspeople. The intermingling of a very personal reaction and the accepted group response to the spectrum of colours is ultimately responsible for originality. The concept of colour was dictated by the term *sofyana rang*. An emphasis on pastel and white shades on a white background was preferred. Fine embroidered work was done in shades discreetly blending with the background while some shawls even today exhibit an inexhaustible display of deep, bright colours. Since the craftsmen had to look beyond the local markets, it was necessary to have a complete range of contrastiing colours which kept changing according to the dictates of the market. In the beginning, the colours favoured were mainly red, saffron and indigo blue. The Central Asian bazaar favoured the deep red colour which is commonly seen in the *kilims* and rugs from this area.

Embroidery is also done on fabrics and garments in the valley. The *pheran* worn by men and women has evolved from a long gown which came into prominence along with a headgear after the Sayyids made their presence felt in the valley. *Pherans*, slightly shorter than those used a century earlier and woven and embroidered with silk or cotton, have invaded the market today. The dominant stitch is chain, while occasionally stem stitch is also

Map shawl of Srinagar; Sri Pratap Singh Museum; Srinagar, Kashmir

A map of Srinagar city done on a pale blue ground. The topography of the city, including the Zabarvan range which encloses it like a bowl, is clearly embroidered at one end of the shawl. The lakes, the decorated *shikaras*, the township on the banks of the river Jhelum, as well as places of religious worship and entertainment, are all depicted. Some of the canals which no longer exist have been clearly marked, along with the military outposts at the base of Hari Parbat. The feeling of a close-knit city is conveyed in this *rumal* which was made in one of the *karkhanas* at Maharaj Ganj. The colours vary from rust brown for the mountains to green for the dense forest. A lighter green is used for the narrow waterways while the Dal and Nagin lakes are a deeper aquamarine.

Major Stuart H. Godfrey exhibited this shawl in 1903 saying, "This specimen of the Kashmir hand-worked shawl was purchased at one of the sales of the surplus shawls of Kashmir held by the Accountant General, J & K State. An account and photograph of this shawl was published in the Magazine of Art in August 1901. The design is a plan scale of the city of Srinagar as it stood in the time of Maharaja Sir Ranbir Singh, GCSI, by whose orders the shawl was made. The shawl was, it is said, designed for presentation to H.M. the King Emperor, then Prince of Wales, had the Royal visit to Jammu extended to Srinagar. The chief places in and around the city can easily be identified from the shawl".

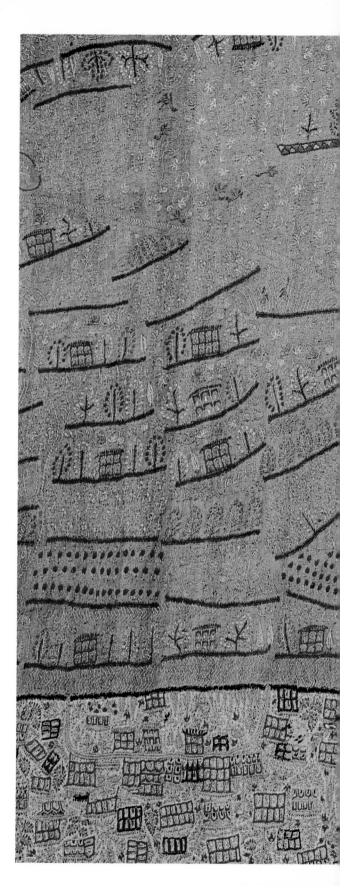

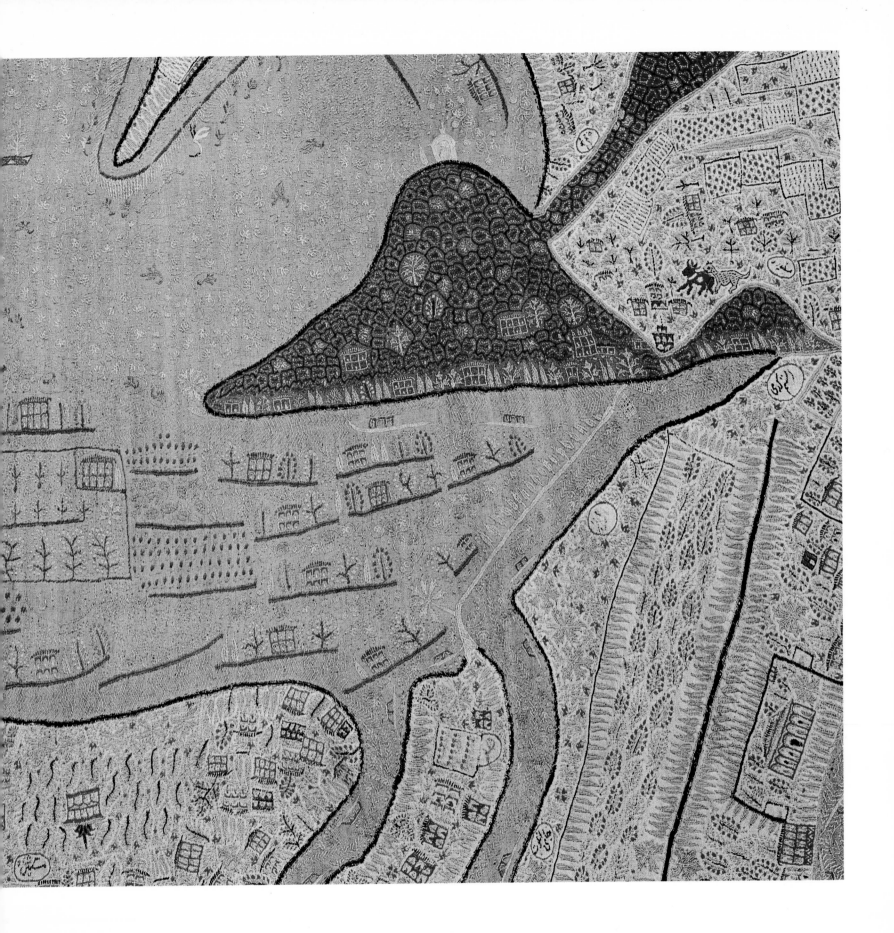

used. Embroidery is done on *raffal* or blended fabrics which is more comfortable in warmer climates.

Kashmiri embroidery is remarkable more for the skilled execution of a single stitch rather than the elaborate quality of the stitch itself. Chain stitch, satin stitch, the slanted darn stitch, stem, herringbone and sometimes the *doori* or knot stitch are used. Excellence in wielding the needle created the *dorukha* in embroidery, in which there is no right and wrong side and the same design is reproduced in different colours on both sides. This technique is executed by splitting the underlying yarn in two with the use of a very fine needle so that the entire fabric is not pierced.

Sozani or fine needlework done by a *sozankar* is the exquisite execution of the darn and herringbone stitch in silk thread used both on the *rumal*, large square head-pieces for the Egyptian market, and shawls for local use. *Vata-chikan*, the buttonhole stitch, is used for filling large spaces. *Amli* shawls employed the minute satin stitch called *chikandozi*, as well the slanted darn and stem stitch. *Zalakdozi* or chain stitch and the *moraskar*, or knot stitch, is executed in metallic or silver thread for a raised or braided effect on the borders of shawls or regal gowns known as *chogas*. The chain stitch was used on a variety of fabrics from hand-woven cloth made from double twisted yarn called *dosooti* to wool, silk and cotton. This is probably the most widely-used stitch as it lent itself to garments, shawls, tapestries and rugs, both for the growing local market as well as the European one.

Chain stitch embroidery employed the use of an *ari*, a small, hooked awl which is believed to have been introduced at the time of the Mughal emperor Akbar. The *ari* is inserted through the cloth in the form of a loop and is finally pulled up through the surface of the cloth to form a stitch. The chain stitch was also used for *gabbas* and *numdahs*, floor coverings used in homes. In the beginning of this century, chain stitch rugs came into vogue. They were the best possible substitutes for carpets and coordinated well with western-style interiors. Slowly, western influence mingled with existing patterns. The floral motif or even copies of miniature paintings done in Mughal times were reproduced on these rugs.

Apart from floral patterns, animal and human figures form the main designs which, as with the shawls, are traced by the *naqash*. The embroidery

Far left

Kashmiri girl wearing a *tilla pheran*

The *pheran* worn by women in the valley has evolved from a long gown. The women wore a fillet around their heads called *kasaba* by the Muslims, and *taranga* by Hindu women. Even now, a *tilla pheran* with exquisite embroidery in gold or silver thread is worn by Muslim brides after the traditional bath. Similarly, a Hindu bride is covered with a shawl on which work is done with gold thread.

Tilla* embroiderer works on a *pheran

The embroiderer keeps the fabric on his knees while he works. For a larger piece, the embroidery is done after the cloth is stretched on a wooden frame. *Zari* thread of either gold or silver is laid upon the fabric, which is wound around the neck of the embroiderer and finally stitched down with a fine matching thread invisible on the surface of the fabric. The colour of the fabric invariably helps in deciding whether the thread should be golden or silver. The *pheran* is embroidered near the neck and shoulders and more lightly at the lower hem and sleeves. Stylised floral motifs and geometric patterns usually embellish the garment.

Dogri bridal *kurta*, and detail, Jammu

A Dogri bridal *kurta* with *gota* applique, sequins and satin ribbon on a grey silk ground. The detail shows stars, circles and various geometrical patterns stitched on the neckline and borders.

work on the material is in woollen yarn of two or three ply and silk yarn is sometimes also used.

A *numdah* is a piece of pressed felt made either out of wool and cotton or entirely of wool. Wool and cotton or unspun wool is evenly spread over a mat and then rolled and pressed underfoot for felting. The felted piece is then milled, washed and dried. Plain as well as embroidered *numdahs* can be seen in Srinagar city being dried in the open by the side of the *nallah* or river. The *numdah* makes a warm, colourful and inexpensive floor covering and is also used as a mattress where the climate is colder.

Originally, the plain *numdah* rug came from Yarkand and was then embroidered in Kashmir. Writing about *numdahs* in *Valley of Kashmir*, Sir Walter Lawrence says, "The best felts are imported from Yarkand but felts of somewhat inferior description are made in Kashmir. The coloured felts embroidered in Srinagar are perhaps the most artistic of Kashmir textiles". *The Gazetteer of Kashmir and Ladakh*, first published in 1890, notes: "Very beautiful and cheap rugs are made of *numdah*, or thick felt. This felt is made in pieces of 1.85 to 2 × 1.3 to 1.5 m. The ground colours are varying shades of brown, fawn, green, blue, yellow etc. The rugs are generally worked all over".

After being made, chain stitch embroidery with woollen yarn is done on the *numdah*, which comes in rectangular, oval or even round shapes. The embroidery is done by hand with a tambour needle or hook. This chain stitch in solid rows with cross fillings in satin and buttonhole stitch is called crewel embroidery and is also applied to furnishing fabric. Traditionally, the *numdah* designs are Kashmir florals.

Though the industry has existed for about 175 years, it was during the Second World War that it got a real impetus. But unhealthy competition among producers led to a terrible deterioration in quality and a setback to the industry between 1947 and 1953.

Exclusive to Kashmir and, more particularly, to the outskirts of Anantnag town and nearby villages the *gabba* or the "common man's carpet" is made of used *lois* or blankets which are washed, milled, and dyed in various colours. *Gabba*-making is a household craft in which family members, especially girls and women, help the male embroiderers in stitching together pieces of used *lois* and giving

Far left

Both sides of *dorukha* or double-faced embroidery in *sozani* on a surface of fine pashmina fabric

The precision and artistry of the Kashmiri embroiderer is best demonstrated in the technique of using a fine needle to split the warp thread of the basic fabric to embroider only its upper half. The underside is left free to be embroidered in another set of colours, repeating the very same design to obtain a reverse mirror image. The same effect is achieved with double sided *ajrakh* printing or *ikat* weaving but these methods cannot boast of the separate colour effect of the famed *dorukha*, or double-faced embroidery.

Cross stitch rug on hessian; contemporary; Srinagar

The Tree of Life is embroidered on a rug with a cluster of medallion-like flowers on the four corners. The cosmic tree is a very common motif used in rugs and tapestries. The tree stands for growth and is symbolic of the flow of life in the world around us. In Kashmir, the *chinar* tree is often depicted on fabrics. While the full tree is embroidered on rugs, only the leaves are represented on shawls.

Embroiderer carrying woolen threads for crewel embroidery

Before carrying the threads home, an embroiderer stops to wash and say his prayers. In the areas surrounding Anantnag in Kashmir, many people are engaged in embroidering pashmina shawls, cotton *dosooti*, *gabbas*, *numdahs* and *raffal*. These are embellished with silken or woollen thread which is purchased from the town bazaar.

Far right

Gabba making, Anantnag; Kashmir

A group of workers from Anantnag chain-stitch a *gabba* in their home. The motifs are selected by the embroiderer from his surroundings and include flowers, vines and birds. Geometric shapes in brilliant primary colours make it more compelling and visually attractive. The *gabba* has red and green diamond-shaped medallions in the centre with a blue-lined trellis border on a red background.

Detail of embroidered *rumal*; contemporary; Jammu

Hanuman, the monkey-god of the *Ramayana,* symbolises loyalty. The art of embroidery in the Jammu region is linked to the hill states and mythological scenes and figures are often worked with thread and needle. Here, silk thread is used in an elongated satin and stem stitch on cotton cloth.

Far right

Chain stitch *rumal*; Sri Pratap Singh Museum; Srinagar, Kashmir

Religious themes were not commonly embroidered. This is an exception which must have been due to the influence of Hindu rulers of the late 19th century, and because of the inflow of ideas from the hill states, where artists excelled in painting scenes from Hindu mythology. The *Ramayana* tells the story of Rama, the seventh incarnation of Vishnu, the preserver, whose wife was abducted by Ravana, King of Lanka. Hanuman, the monkey-god known for his loyalty to Rama, is shown with his hands folded before Rama and Sita, waited upon by three attendants in the background. The chain stitch is worked in silk thread on cotton cloth.

them a backing of waste cotton cloth. Some girls have also recently taken to embroidering *gabbas*. Washing and dyeing is done indigenously.

There are two types of *gabbas* — embroidered and appliqued. Bold and vivid embroidery is done mostly in woollen yarn. In some cheaper types of *gabbas*, cotton yarn is used instead. In the appliqued type, pieces of dyed blankets are joined together and interspersed with embroidery. *Gabbas* look very gay with bright flashes of designs on a dark, sombre background.

The origin of the appliqued type of *dal-guldar gabba* is not known but there are several interesting anecdotes. One of them is that Abdul Rahman, a refugee from Kabul, prepared an appliqued saddle piece for his host, Kamal Dutt of Tetson village near Tral. This saddle piece was greatly appreciated and the idea caught on with the *gabba* makers in Anantnag. During Dogra rule, Maharaja Ranbir Singh gave a fillip to the *gabba* craft when he invited craftsmen to prepare *shamianas*, *kanats* and *gabbas* for state use. The use of *banat* or broad cloth instead of old *lois* improved the value and appearance of special *gabbas* patronised by the palace.

Since the industry is concentrated in rural areas the *gabba* has a comparatively folk flavour. Kashmiris use *gabbas* for picnics, as ordinary floor spreads and as colourful mattresses, which are properly lined, filled with cotton, quilted and piped to match the *gabbas*. However, the *gabba* craft is now losing its earlier characteristics. Instead of the use of waste material, barrack blankets, which are easier to work on, are increasingly being used.

Both 19th century Kashmir and the Jammu region adjoining Himachal share the embroidery style of the Chamba *rumals*. Mythological figures and scenes, animals and birds are embroidered vertically, horizontally or in a circular form on square pieces. They demonstrate the effect of Hindu origins combined with the skill of both Muslim craftsmen and Jammu craftswomen to create elaborate and colourful pictures in bright silk floss thread.

Deft fingers holding a needle still signify the artistry of the embroiderers from this region and reiterate the notion that a man or woman with imagination and skill needs only the simplest of implements to create patterns of infinite beauty.

Far left

Floral motif in chain stitch, detail; Srinagar, Kashmir

Floral, animal and leaf patterns are widely used in most Kashmiri craft. This detail from a chain stitch rug shows the use of a fine awl and woollen thread. The tightly laid out concentric circles add liveliness to the motifs they encompass.

***Numdah* maker drying embroidered rugs on a *karkhana* rooftop; Srinagar, Kashmir**

Once the felt is pounded into shape, it is embroidered with woollen threads in chain stitch. Most designs are floral and contemporary in style, although traditional motifs such as the *chinar* leaf, local flowers and the kingfisher are also widely used.

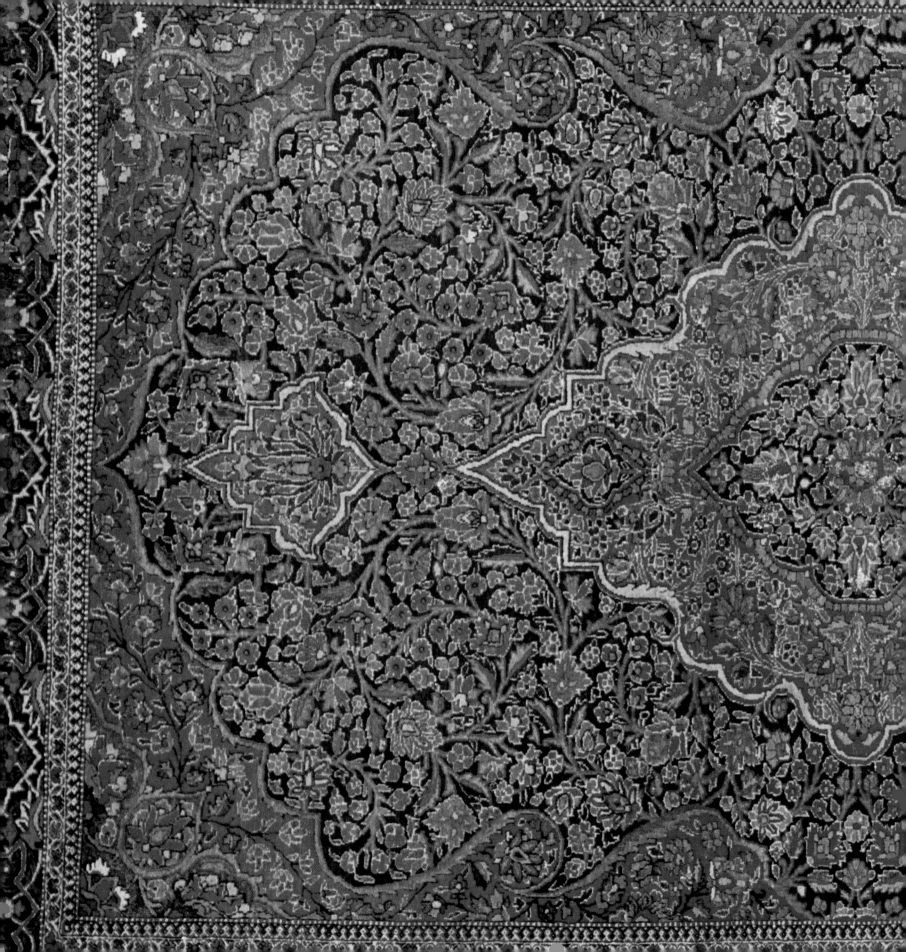

Carpets

While the origin of hand-knotted carpets in the world can be traced back more than 2,000 years, in India the craft was first introduced in Kashmir in the 15th century after which it progressively attained a high degree of perfection. It is said that Sultan Zain-ul-Abadin brought carpet weavers from Persia and Central Asia into Kashmir to train the local inhabitants and since spinning and weaving was already being practised there from very early times, carpet weaving soon developed.

Sultan Zain-ul-Abadin's introduction of *karkhanas* or factories for carpet weavers enabled the craft to flourish but after his reign, the lack of enlightened patronage resulted in carpet weaving gradually becoming extinct. It witnessed a revival only in Emperor Jehangir's time.

As the story goes, an eminent scholar and saint, Akhun Mulla Rahnuma, revived the industry with the help of Ahmed Beg Khan, Governor of Kashmir between 1614-1618. Ahmed Khan, it is said, acquired the knowledge of various techniques at Andijan in Persia, on his way back from his pilgrimage to Mecca and also brought back with him the

tools of the trade. Imported skill and imperial patronage helped to develop the craft again during the Mughal period.

During this time, *karkhanas* entered a new phase that subsequently manifested itself in a money economy and the system of wages changed from payment in kind, like salt and tea, to cash. During the reign of the Mughals each *karkhana* was headed by a *vasta-ustad*, master craftsman, who supervised the work of the *tsats*, craftsmen, and *shagirds*, apprentices. All craftsmen working in the trade were called *kalbaf*. The *vasta-ustad* was the supervisor and the main link between the artisans and entrepreneurs.

The Mughal reign was followed by Afghan and Sikh rule, a highly unsettled period for Kashmir, during which the *karkhana* system of carpet weaving as well as other crafts declined. Precipitated by mechanised imitations in England and the Franco-Prussian war, Kashmir's shawl industry also collapsed and left a number of weavers, who were already in a miserable condition, further destitute.

But the fortuitous development of the carpet industry during Maharaja Ranbir Singh's time (1857-1885) led to an enhancement of carpet production, both in terms of quantity and quality. However, the social status of the weavers did not improve correspondingly.

The display of two exceptionally beautiful Mughal carpets at the Great Crystal Palace Exhibition, London, in 1857, caught the imagination of the West and helped create an awareness and appreciation for Kashmir carpets in western markets. Carpet weaving subsequently got a fresh impetus in Kashmir after European companies including Mitchell and Co., the East India Carpet Company and C.M. Hadow and Co., established organised factories. Some local entrepreneurs also took to the craft later and began exporting carpets to Great Britain, France and other European countries, Canada and the U.S.A. in the beginning of the twentieth century.

In the early 1920s, however, due to world recession, the carpet trade received a debilitating setback with the result that most of the carpet factories in Kashmir closed down. The export market picked up during the following decade and this lasted till the beginning of the Second World War. Both the war and the partition of India dealt the

industry a serious blow as it lost both internal and overseas markets and a few of the pioneers left Kashmir permanently. In 1950, with the concerted efforts of a few manufacturers, the industry was re-established and since then it has made tremendous progress.

While carpet weaving, *kalbafi*, is still looked down upon socially and weavers' children prefer to turn to other occupations, there has been some improvement in the last four decades. The introduction of new designs, the establishment of training programmes in rural areas and the encouragement given by official agencies to women to enter the profession have created a fairly widespread population of new carpet weavers, for whom a more generous recognition of their fine skills and consequent higher wages have brought a more elevated status in society. However, they still need financial and marketing support before they can evolve to be confident, growing and self-sufficient members of the craft society.

Today, there are about a dozen organised *karkhanas*, each employing over 100 weavers at one place, besides entrusting work to other small units. The system of wages is per thousand knots and the weaving is done under supervision. These *karkhanas* maintain their own designing and drafting sections, dyeing and washing arrangements, and also have their main showrooms on the premises. While a weaver is a full-time worker in the city, the new entrants in rural areas are part-time weavers who combine the craft with their agricultural jobs. Usually, the weaver is attached to a manufacturer or dealer and has to depend on these businessmen for orders as well as raw materials. The design is indicated to him by those who place the orders. With the exception of a few master weavers, very few craftsmen choose their own designs.

The hours of work in earlier days can be deduced from the adage, *bange atsun te tasanyi narun* ("to start early in the morning when Muslims are called for prayer and to stop very late in the evening when lamps are lit").

Today, the wages of a good carpet weaver average Rs.20-25 per day against Rs.2 or thereabouts which was the rate before India became independent. The demand for carpets has vastly increased in recent years, as have their prices. The

Previous page

Mohtashan Kashan; size: 130 cms × 194 cms; quality: 360 (18/20) knots per square inch

Reproduction of Mohtashan Kashan (also spelt *mochtchan*, meaning lamb's wool), a well-known Persian design. The classic medallion with an elegant motif above and below lend the carpet a majestic look, enriched by fine flowers in the centre field with a corresponding floral border. The corners are also decorated with floral motifs. In Kashmir it is said that the Mohtashan design is named after the family of its original weaver.

Syrk Turkoman; size: 145 cms × 184 cms; quality: 165 (11/15) knots per square inch

Reproduction of an antique Syrk rug named after the tribe who first wove it in Turkoman. In the early days it was mostly used as tent-door drapery or a wall-hanging. The design is a latchhook pattern on a mahogany coloured background. The central rectangle suggests two *mehrabs*, arches, one above the other. There is a hem on the upper side, and a *kilim* (pileless weaving) and fringe at the bottom. The weft and warp are in wool.

price in 1956-57 for a quality 196 (14 × 14) knots per square inch woollen carpet was Rs.15 per square foot, against Rs.2,000 today. The wages for staple rayon silk carpets, which now form the bulk of production, are less than Rs.100 per square foot in 284 (18 × 18) quality while the wage for a pure silk carpet is Rs.112. The former is easier and faster to weave. The difference in cost of material is over ten times. Staple is Rs.50 per kg., while silk is Rs.500 per kg. In Kashmiri carpets, the ratio of raw material to wages is generally 30:70.

Carpets from 200 knots to 900 knots per square inch both in wool and silk yarn have attained such excellence that today they rank among the finest in the world. Kashmir has also begun making *zari* carpets, with metallic threads in the warp, and the Shab-i-Charag carpet, which is embedded with pearls reflects the light of a candle in a dark room.

But there have also been certain unhealthy developments such as the mass production of carpets which lack even the minimum devotion to quality. Traders from other parts of the country and others who know nothing about carpets have entered the business with just one asset — money. Consequently, there has been a glut of low-grade carpets due to which the industry has suffered both losses as well as damage to its reputation. However, the market for fine-quality Kashmir carpets sustains skilled craftsmanship and a good wage structure.

There has been a steady growth of production in artificial silk carpets which is considered an undesirable development responsible for introducing an element of synthetic artificiality into the famed high-value carpet of pure material as well as leaving the field open for dishonest substitution of pure silk by artificial silk.

The loom used in Kashmir carpet weaving is composed of two horizontal wooden beams between which the warp threads are stretched, one beam in front of the weaver and the second behind the first. The difference between a carpet and other hand-loom textiles lies in the fact that short lengths of thread or yarn are tied to warp chains to form the pile of the carpets. These are commonly called 'knots' though it is a loop rather than an actual knot.

There are different types of knots and in Kashmir

Detail of *zari* and silk *shikargah* carpet; quality: 400 (20/20) knots (double) per square inch

The design, copied from a Mughal painting, depicts princes hunting in a jungle. Very few master carpet weavers know the art of weaving *zari* into a carpet. The carpet shows Mughal princes on horseback engaged in fighting with lions, leopards, hyenas and other animals, vividly bringing out the embossed effect. The embossing is done while the carpet is on the loom. The work of a great master craftsman, this carpet took 16 months to weave.

the Farsi *baff* and the Persian system known as the Sehna, or Sinneh, knot are generally used. The Sehna knot consists of one end of the thread being looped around a warp chain to emerge between the second warp chain and the chain that will carry the loop in the following knot.

The knot can be tied around four warp threads by taking up two at a time. This is called the *jufti* or double knot and while it allows knotting to progress more rapidly, it also affects the beauty and life of the carpet.

Very simple tools are used to make carpets in Kashmir. These include a blade to make the initial cut once the thread has been knotted, a wood or metal comb to push knots and weft tightly together, and a pair of short scissors to cut the carpet to an even form once it is finished.

The larger the number of knots the higher the quality, is the general criterion for evaluating carpets, and fine knotting makes it possible to depict the smallest motif with precision. But this factor has been overstressed for there can be excellent carpets with a low number of knots per square inch. The raw material, dyeing, beauty and delicacy of design, fine workmanship and excellence in finish are all factors which contribute towards quality. The border is also very important as it determines the strength of a carpet. Carpets in 18 × 18 and 20 × 20 knots per square inch are commonly made in Kashmir these days. Some very fine silk carpets in small sizes have been created with knots as high as 3,600 per square inch but these rare exhibitions of skill are mainly made for display or as museum pieces.

Till the 1860s, carpets in Kashmir were made with colours extracted from vegetable or animal sources. The people of Asia were experts in the art of dyeing and the results of their artistry provided an extremely subtle yet luminous range of colours.

Dyes were made in the homes of the craftsmen. The madder root, which grew wild, provided the most important range of pinks and reds, and cochineal and turmeric were also used for shades of red. The saffron crocus, cultivated in the fields of Pampore in Kashmir, provided pure yellow, while its wild counterpart, as well as pomegranate skin and distilled turmeric, provided reddish yellow. The rhubarb plant is said to provide dark red and cop-

per red. Green came from the grass (*Kusa*) and brown from the leaves of the *kikar* tree.

Aniline dyes, which are easier to procure and use, were introduced a little over a century ago. But they compare poorly to vegetable dyes and have a tendency to fade much quicker, with carpets taking on a flat, greyish colour after a few years. The chrome dyeing process, however, ensures that the colours are fixed better.

Writing about dyes, E. Gans Roedin, a researcher on carpets, says, "When one contemplates on early carpets, the pile is brought to life with an interplay of infinite reflections... it is impossible to achieve such an alluring sheen with chemically dyed wool."

George Birdwood, who documented the industrial arts in the 19th century, echoes the same sentiment: "The industry has been revived," he wrote, "and the carpets now produced under European supervision do not fail to satisfy a critical taste. The manufacture of carpets is capable of great extension and has a great future before it, if only somehow aniline dyes could be kept out of the country."

The carpet industry in Kashmir is known to be mainly of Persian origin. Iran produces carpets of varying qualities in different parts of the country, ranging from the coarser tribal carpets from Hamedan, Shiraz and Abade to the fine high quality silk and wool carpets from Isfahan, Kashan, Mesched, Sarook and Kirman. Kashmir, however, only received the best court traditions of Iran and from the beginning the finest quality carpets were woven in the valley, embodying the best designs of the Shah Abbas tradition. The designs in Kashmir have always been comparable to the best in Persia and in technique, virtuosity and skill there are craftsmen in Kashmir who can even today match the best production of their ancestors.

While the designs and patterns in Kashmir carpets these days continue to be mainly inspired by Persian carpets and Central Asian rugs, the influence of the region's flora and fauna has remained. "Some arrangements give an image of the tranquil beauty of the Kashmir countryside," observed Albrecht Hope, an authority on Oriental carpets. Flowers native to Kashmir have been incorporated in a number of Persian designs. In the *gamla* or vase design with its flowering branches, "sprays of flowers of many forms and colours burst like fire-

Carpet weaver, Srinagar

A carpet weaver is seen behind the warp from the other side of the loom. Many young persons receive training with master weavers and today represent a major part of the carpet weaving community.

works," while the *khatirast*, a design of narrow stripes or bands with flowers ranged alongside is another speciality of Kashmir.

Oriental rugs generally use symbolic motifs: the circle denotes eternity; the zigzag motif water and light; the swastika symbolises light showing the way in darkness; the meander denotes the continuity of life; and the tree stands for happiness and goodness. Traditional Persian patterns were often made up of various floral motifs such as the rose, lotus, poppy, myrtle, crocus, narcissus, lily, the Tree of Life and a variety of birds.

The Kashmiri carpet weaver takes special pride in his ability to accurately reproduce old Persian carpets. An Iranian masterpiece — the celebrated Ardebil Mosque carpet made in 1536 by the artist Maqsud of Kashan and now owned by the South Kensington Museum in London — was reproduced in Kashmir in 1902. The main design comprises a large central medallion in pale yellow surrounded by cartouches of various colours set off against a dark blue background dispersed with floral tracery. Each corner of the carpet is filled with the section of a large medallion surrounded by cartouches. The border is composed of long and circular panels alternating with lobed outlines on a brown background embellished with floral motifs.

Besides reproducing Persian, Turkish, Turkoman and Caucasian patterns, carpets have been made with Kashmiri and Mughal patterns and in the early 1960s, carpets with *amlikar* shawl patterns were introduced. One such carpet was presented to the Queen of England by the Indian government.

Many carpets demonstrate the genius of modern Kashmir carpet designers who preserve the essence of ancient patterns while adapting them to contemporary demands. This can be seen in the gentle tones of a carpet's pattern and structure. A typical Kashmiri creation is the *boteh-meiri* or princely flower motif, which is reminiscent of the traditional Kashmir shawl.

Kashmiri rugs are known for their wealth of colours and shades and the scenic splendour of the land is a perennial source of inspiration for its designers and craftsmen. The colours in Kashmir carpets do not normally stand in contrast to one another, but are carefully graded. Besides their aesthetic sophistication and harmony, the variety of colours offer flexibility of use in modern interiors.

Carpet weaver tying a knot between the two warp cotton threads

The craftsman holds a curved knife in his right hand, with which he cuts the woollen yarn hanging from above after the knot has been tied. A comb is used to beat in the weft and pile tufts and a pair of scissors smoothens the pile level. These simple tools and an upright wooden loom of traditional design are all that is needed to combine with the skill and dexterity of the carpet weaver.

Far right

Kashmir Qum (also called Ghoum); size: 100 cms × 180 cms; quality: 400 (20/20) knots per square inch

Persian in origin, the design consists of assorted panels with various motifs, which are repeated. The four corners in this particular carpet have an unusually prominent motif. In Qum carpets one comes across a wide variety of motifs, harmoniously arranged to create a mosaic of panels.

Following page

Turkoman Princess Bukhara; quality: 126 (9/14) knots per square inch

Section of an antique Turkoman Princess Bukhara design, also known as Hetchulu, which has been successfully reproduced in Kashmir. The design is based on a candle-stick-holder pattern on an old brick red background. The original carpet was woven in yarn dyed in vegetable colours.

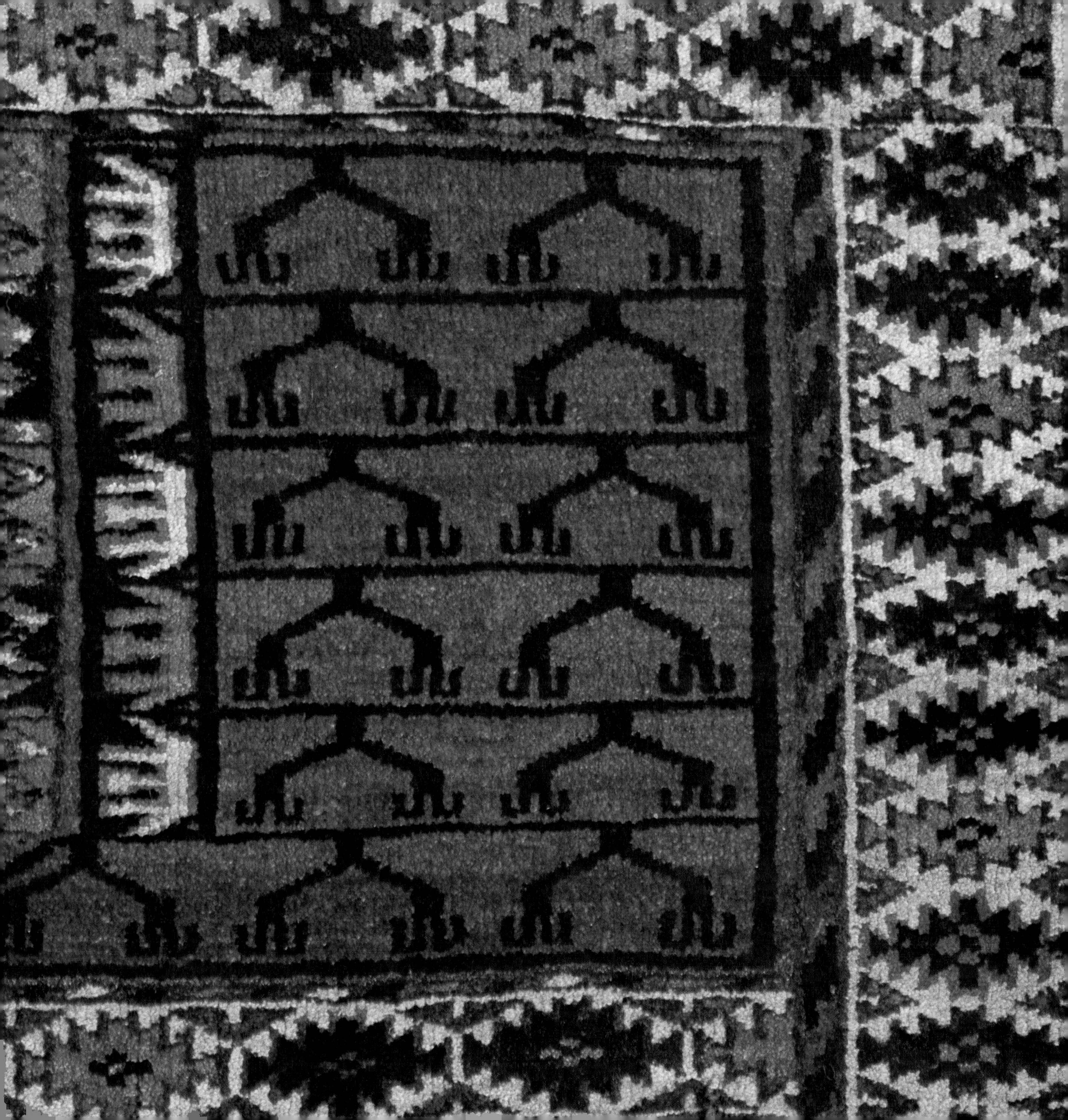

Kashmir carpet designs are usually written down on paper in a kind of shorthand style called *talim*, a practice derived from the traditional methods used for making *kani* shawls. When the shawl weavers turned to carpet weaving they continued the practice of following the *talim*. This method spread even to Amritsar in the Punjab when some weavers moved there from Kashmir.

In the Kashmir carpet industry there is a class of persons called *talim* writers who prepare the *talim* from a design worked out on graph paper. The number of *talim* writers in Kashmir has not kept pace with the growth of carpet weaving and efforts at training young persons in the art are under way. A roll of paper is marked with a code indicating the number of knots to be woven in each colour selected for the carpet. Preparing a *talim* calls for care and experience. The design on the graph paper is divided into squares of 25 compartments, each representing one knot that is marked on the *talim*. The colours are matched with the code. For a carpet measuring 300 × 200 cms, with a knot count of 570,000 per square yard, 200 strips of paper will be used for a design with a central medallion and 800 for a continuous pattern. Copies of a *talim* are made by hand and several carpets of a particular design can be made on different looms at the same time.

A senior weaver reads out — almost singing — the *talim* to his fellow workers and often the *ustad*, master craftsman, recites a pattern that he has memorised through practice. Sitting with their knees upwards, at least two or three young boys with the master weaver at the head of the loom, knot a carpet, sometimes chanting a reply to indicate that they have complied with the instructions. The atmosphere in the *karkhana* is suggestive of work and pleasure together. After every few inches of knotting, the carpet is rolled over the lower beam of the loom and the *talim*, which is fixed into the warp threads, is raised slightly.

The last 40 years have seen a great upsurge of interest in Oriental carpets, rugs and flat weaves and the market for hand-knotted carpets has grown significantly in West Europe, the U.S. and West Asia. There has been a corresponding rise in competition from China and Pakistan. But Kashmir's rich tradition of skill, knowledge and designs remain great assets and constitute a firm basis for

Far left

Kashmir Mughal; size: 100 cms × 153 cms; quality: 400 (20/20) knots per square inch

In a striking reproduction of a 17th century Mughal design the chrysanthemum motif stands out prominently on a camel-coloured background with a red border. The arch with a lighter background highlights the central arrangement. The carpet has a silk warp and weft.

Jaipur Mughal; size: 122 cms × 184 cms; quality: 324 (18/18) knots per square inch

Reproduction of an antique Jaipur Mughal design, in the form of compartments on a red background. The bouquets with rose-shaped flowers ornament the medallions and the rosettes occupy the borders, intertwined with small buds. The carpet combines a bold geometric and floral effect.

the future growth in production of finely knotted carpets. One drawback, however, is that Kashmir presently lacks sufficient dyeing and washing facilities.

In the desert plateau of Ladakh, which is bordered on the east by Tibet, a style of carpet weaving similar to the Tibetan one is practised. This tradition is essentially Central Asian and differs from that followed in the Kashmir valley.

The Ladakhis weave carpets on an easily portable, vertical loom. The warp is prepared from cotton and stretched on the frame. The looping of the woollen yarn is initiated by introducing a long iron rod around which the wool is looped and attached to the warp threads. The threads used vary in diameter from 75 cms to one cm, depending on the thickness of the pile required. Different coloured wool is introduced to produce the desired pattern. After each weft row is completed, the loops are cut with a sharp knife and the rod removed and this process continues till the entire carpet is woven. After being completed, the carpet is trimmed with clipping scissors to make the design motifs more conspicuous.

In Ladakh, carpets which are known as *khabdan*, are generally woven in sizes of 61 cms × 168 cms. The cotton warp is invariably of 6/6 quality count and the woollen yarn 2.5 mm in diameter. Carpets made in this area are distinct not only in the technique used but also in their designs. Some of the most popular motifs done in glowing colours include the *druk*, dragon; snow lion, *cha*, and birds and florals, *mentok*, such as a stylised chrysanthemum or lotus.

Carpet patterns are also derived from the *tashistatz gyat*, a composition of auspicious symbols in Buddhist iconography. The eight auspicious signs include *tung*, the conch shell; *spalpio*, endless knot; *sernya*, pair of golden fish; *padma*, the lotus; *gyaltsan*, the banner of victory; *khorlo*, the wheel of religion; *dug*, the umbrella or canopy; and *pumpa*, the holy vase. Interesting geometric patterns are also made using ultramarine, brown, white and yellow, with the border in diagonal lines. The borders of Ladakhi carpets usually depict the *gyanakchagri*, a Chinese wall motif and the configuration of stylised border lines draws its inspiration from the famous Great Wall of China.

Kashmir Kashan; size: 130 × 194 cms; quality: 361 (19/19) knots per square inch

The design depicts a Tree of Life with delicate flowers in bloom. Along with flowers, animals and birds are also sometimes introduced in Kashmir Kashans. This carpet has four stags at the lower end of the central field, while four birds nestle symmetrically among the flowers on either side of the central branch.

Far left

Women weavers at the loom; Ladakh

In Ladakh the carpets have a distinctly Tibetan influence. They are made on the traditional loom and employ motifs such as the dragon and lotus. The pattern is followed directly from a graph as the *talim* tradition is unknown. Women have been trained to weave very recently.

Section of an old Tibetan/Ladakh carpet

The entire carpet consists of a long strip of three similar sections with medallions. The border around them is called *gyanakchagri* (Chinese wall). The colours used are vegetable dyes, including indigo. Such carpets are used in monasteries by lamas during their prayers.

A type of carpet woven particularly in the Chang Thang area of Ladakh is known as *tsukdan*. In this carpet both the warp and weft are of yak wool and the year long cold necessitates this type of warm floor covering. People seat their guests on the *tsukdan* and spread it out for ceremonies and feasts.

Another carpet from Ladakh, known as the *tsuktul*, is woven in small, 20 cm widths of running lengths. After being woven, these strips are stitched together to form a 155 cms × 170 cms carpet whose pile is generally one cm. This is used both as a floor-spread as well as a heavy blanket. The woollen yarn — known for providing luxurious warmth — is spun from the wool of local sheep.

Thus, as we have seen, the northern Himalayan region of India still holds its own among the best known carpets of the world and the carpet weaver is intensely proud of his skill and international renown.

Yak wool floor covering, Mulbekh, Ladakh

Yak wool is woven into narrow strips interspersed with sections of bright colours with common knitting wool. The pile gives warmth to this covering which also serves as a blanket.

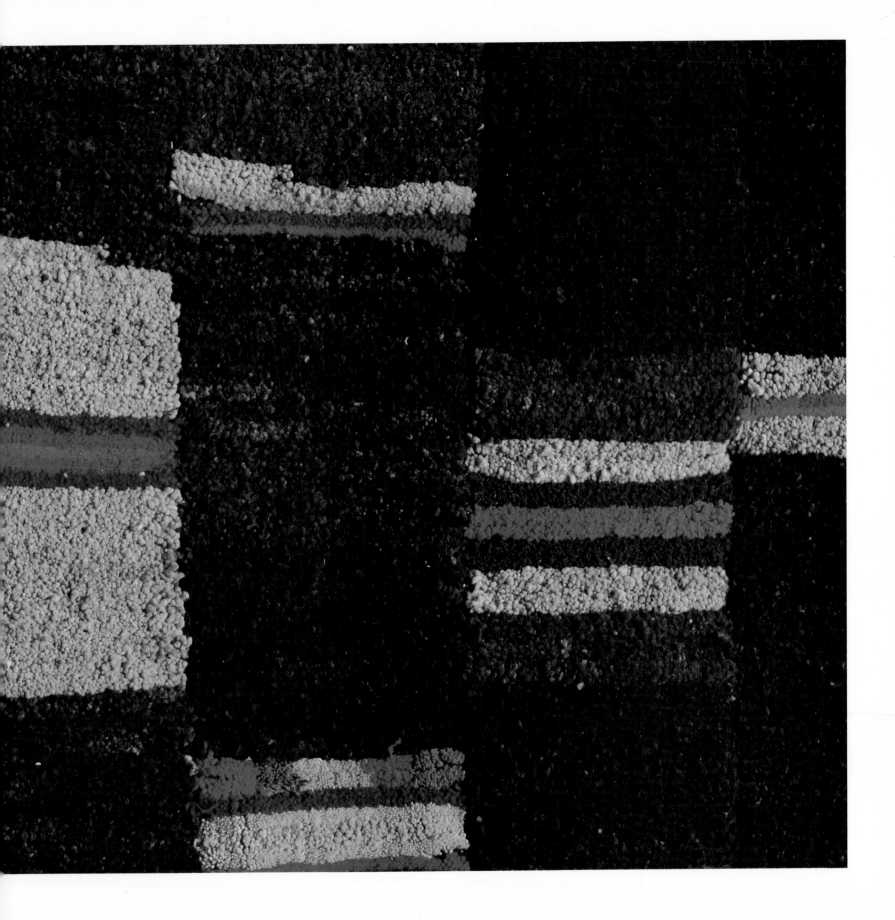

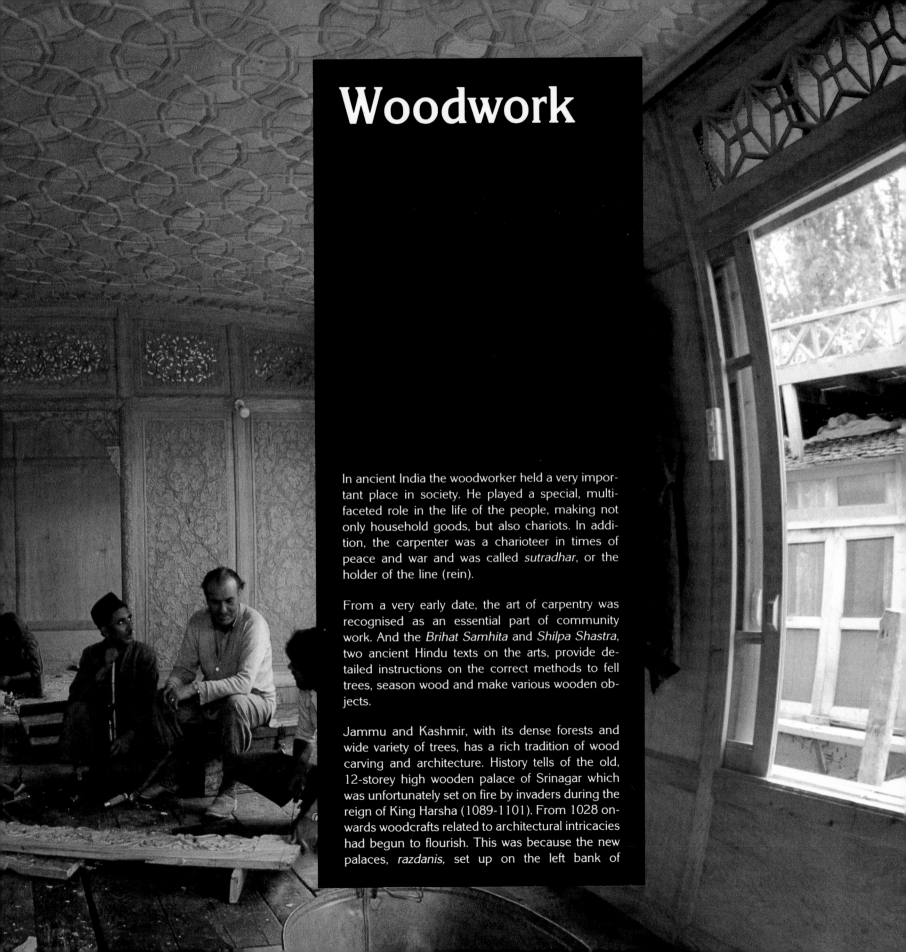

Woodwork

In ancient India the woodworker held a very important place in society. He played a special, multi-faceted role in the life of the people, making not only household goods, but also chariots. In addition, the carpenter was a charioteer in times of peace and war and was called *sutradhar*, or the holder of the line (rein).

From a very early date, the art of carpentry was recognised as an essential part of community work. And the *Brihat Samhita* and *Shilpa Shastra*, two ancient Hindu texts on the arts, provide detailed instructions on the correct methods to fell trees, season wood and make various wooden objects.

Jammu and Kashmir, with its dense forests and wide variety of trees, has a rich tradition of wood carving and architecture. History tells of the old, 12-storey high wooden palace of Srinagar which was unfortunately set on fire by invaders during the reign of King Harsha (1089-1101). From 1028 onwards woodcrafts related to architectural intricacies had begun to flourish. This was because the new palaces, *razdanis*, set up on the left bank of

the river Vitasta or Jhelum were close to the rich forests of Tashwan. These were well-known forests at that time and offered plenty of pine for construction. Although the expansive valley forests have met the same fate as the cedar forests of Lebanon the areas between the Jhelum river and the Kutkol canal are still known as Kathul or Kathleshwar and Tashwan.

It was King Ananta (1028-1063) who moved the traditional royal palace on the right bank to its present location on the left bank between Purshyar, near the Second Bridge and the Kutkol canal. The great height, excellence and majesty of these wooden architectural edifices are specially referred to by the great 11th century Kashmiri author and poet Bilhana, in his famous courtly epic *Vikramankadeva Charitam*. It was in this region that King Jayasimha (1128-1140) allowed his citizens a free supply of forest wood, thus enabling wooden houses to be built in the whole area.

This tradition of wooden architecture and craft reached its excellence between 1420 and 1470, when King Zain-ul-Abadin built his *razdani* which testified to the richness of the heritage. Unfortunately, this artistic edifice along with the *zaina dub*, the great balcony on the topmost floor, was set alight by Chak rebels and apparently kept smouldering for a whole year.

In this region, where wood was used by king, peasant and boatman to make homes, domestic utensils and decorative objects, specific methods of using wood for different purposes were developed. In *khatumband*, for instance, a woodcraft unique to Kashmir, excellent joinery and precise designing combine to create patterned ceiling panels. Thin sheets of wood, usually from a kind of spruce (*Picea webbina*), are held together by double-grooved battens. The wooden sheets are cut into geometric shapes using a template to ensure that the pieces can be interchanged. These modules are fitted into the grooves of the battens and a repeat pattern is built up. Some of the finest examples of *khatumband* ceilings can be seen in the wooden shrines of Naqshband in Srinagar and Nund Rishi in Chirar-e-Sharif.

The renowned lattice-work of Kashmir known as *acchi-dar* and *zali-pinjra* also display remarkable carpentry skills. *Zali-pinjra* is a recent term and refers to the network of intersecting lines which makes up latticed panels, chiefly as a decorative architectural feature.

In authentic *pinjra* work, glue and nails are never used; the extremely thin laths of wood are held together by the pressure they exert on each other. Certain main laths are held together by wooden screws and additional pressure is exerted by the outer frame of the panel. Really good *pinjra* work remains intact even when the frame is removed. The wood used is usually from the deodar tree (*Cedrus libani, var. deodara*) which is especially popular among woodworkers in Kashmir because it is abundantly available and, interestingly, contains an insect-repellant.

While *khatumband* and *pinjra* are very old forms of Kashmiri wood craft, the art of carving decorative boxes, screens and panels of walnut wood appears to be a more recent innovation, at least on the scale on which it is conducted. The shawl trade and the popularity of papier maché and other valley crafts in Europe seem to have given a strong incentive to woodcarvers of the early 20th century. Encouraged by the enthusiasm and suggestions of European traders, the carvers soon reached a stage where they vied with each other to produce more and more elaborate work. The chief characteristic of this was the amount of difficult undercutting, or cutting away of portions of the wood beneath the main pattern. The strong, rich, dark and grainy wood of the walnut tree (*Juglans regia*), known as *dun* in Kashmiri, was considered ideal for this carved work though it was not easy to procure.

Most historical accounts of the crafts of Kashmir lament the coming of age of walnut wood carving, as most of its products reflected the worst kind of European influence — a laboured realism and a tendency to embellish purely for a dramatic display of skill. Percy Brown, commenting in 1909 on the carved pears, water lilies and *chinar* leaves on walnut boxes and furniture, said that these showed a "marvellous degree of undercutting and corresponding loss of art feeling". Nevertheless, walnut wood carving cannot be dismissed for it reveals the dexterity of the Kashmiri wood carver and some of the finest examples are truly breathtaking. One of the most celebrated pieces of work in walnut is the entrance gate built at the time of the Delhi Durbar for King George V's coronation in 1910. This gate incorporated intricate carving in floral motifs and lattice work in geometric patterns.

Previous page

Typical houseboat interior being made with *khatumband* panels

Although boat making is technically different from architectural construction, the need for modern luxuries has resulted in the two techniques being combined, as in the case of a modern houseboat. The construction of the hull, the basic floating body, is done by a separate group of artisans and this is superimposed with a series of cabins and lounges which are panelled and decorated with *khatumband* joinery and carved facades. In the foreground, a *khatumband* carpenter prepares the strips which, when grooved together, form a unit of designs that is repeated on a ceiling or a wall panel.

Brick and wood house; 18th century; Rainawari, Srinagar

This four-storeyed house, reflected in the canal waters which lead to the famous Nagin lake, is an ideal example of the combination of brick and wood. The brickwork, mostly employed in the first three storeys, provides an excellent frame for the woodwork windows while the projecting balcony, flanked with an all-round gallery, adds to the majesty of the building. The house is a typical specimen of 18th century architecture in which the wooden pile system gave way to the total employment of bricks. The woodwork was used mainly for windows, balconies and roofs.

In the forewaters of the canal the front portion of a *bahat*, a typical cargo-boat, shows the continuance of the traditional transport system.

Naqshband mosque, Srinagar

This typical wooden arch is filled with intricate carvings of various motifs and several panels are fitted within the framework. These panels have tree motifs whose details resemble the rococo style of the Washkar school. The existence of ornately carved pendants on both sides of the arch are reminiscent of the traditional eave hangings which were used in ancient and medieval wooden architecture.

Far right

Shrine of Nund Rishi, Chirar-e-Sharif, Kashmir

The exterior of the shrine is a typical combination of various woodcraft techniques employed in early medieval architecture. The hanging decorative eaves are formed by a single cut-work unit arranged together in a repetitive manner. The projecting eaves are supported by a series of brackets which are among the finest examples of Kashmiri woodcraft. The triangular formation is obtained through the manipulation of a decorative branch that is based on a round pedestal with a series of tapering rings. The top-end of each bracket has a lathe-turned decorative hanging reminiscent of later hangings at eave-corners of medieval architecture. The arches are interspersed with tapering pillars with the tree motif and mounted on the capital which is decorated with a series of strips of various running patterns. The projecting side and front facade are ideal depictions of a floral unit that becomes an all-over repetitive pattern. A lack of appreciation of exquisite workmanship is discernible in the electric bulbs fixed over the carvings and decorations in recent times.

Percy Brown tells us that, according to tradition in Rangoon and Peshawar, various forms of woodwork evolved from the complex craft of boat-making. This is also likely to have happened in Jammu and Kashmir where boating and boat-making have always been an essential part of daily life. Some of the major roads connecting the big towns of the region were only built in the 20th century, till when almost all commercial and private traffic was dependent on boats.

To serve various needs, at least ten different types of flat-bottomed boats were regularly manufactured in Kashmir. Generally, planks of cedar and punt-poles of deodar were used for large barges. The boats varied from the *bahats*, a long barge with a two-roomed cabin for the boatman and his family, capable of holding upto 30 tonnes of grain, to the sleek and fast-moving *parinda*, or "flyer", in which upto four passengers sit under a canopy, while 40 to 50 paddlers propel them along the waters, displaying fancy strokes controlled by the slightest movement of the wrist. The most common passenger boat is the *dunga*, about 20 metres in length and two metres wide. The *dunga* has two cabins, one for the boatman and his family, the other for passengers. Both cabins have a sloping roof and walls of woven *waggu* matting. A very small boat, the *dembnao*, was a vital link between communities in the past regularly supplying vegetables to small villages. The older houseboats are treasure troves of Kashmiri woodwork and many boast *khatumband* ceilings and elaborate carvings.

The earliest reference to such a boat is contained in the *Ain-e-Akbari* which records the construction of "a model of a ship" under Emperor Akbar's orders and was an attempt to introduce a design from the eastern parts of the country. On a visit to Kashmir, it is said that the emperor was unimpressed by the appearance of the local boats and wanted them to be constructed in the shape and design he had seen in Bengal. Consequently, this model was quickly constructed and the river Vitasta was soon crowded with them. As late as in the 19th century, W. Wakefield, who wrote *The History of Kashmir and Kashmiris*, records that the "model of a ship" was called *bangala*, after the place of its origin. What the original model looked like, and how far the influence of Bengal actually combined with local traditions, is still unknown.

The woodwork of Anantnag and Kulgam *tehsils*, in

Naqshband mosque, external facade, Srinagar

A typical specimen of a later architectural pile system which was interspersed with brick fittings. The specified repetitive motif in the eave line shows the process of eliminating representational motifs and indicates a degeneration of style. The decorative floral pendants at the eave-corners have also been reduced in size and the representational character of motifs narrowed down. The brackets supporting the eaves have also become simpler than those of the Nund Rishi shrine at Chirar-e-Sharif. In contrast to the bold pile system, very delicate latticework windows are encased within the entire interior wall. Using the *punj pehlu* pattern in latticework ideally matches the pile system and is one of the simplest designs in the craft vocabulary.

Interior of Nund Rishi mosque, Chirar-e-Sharif, Kashmir

This mosque is a typical example of Kashmir's medieval wooden architecture and is built with the crisscross pile system of round or roughly chopped rectangular logs of deodar wood. In a later development, the hollow spaces formed by the pile were filled in with small, baked bricks. The external facade of the mosque is a typical example of this system. The interior of the mosque demonstrates the finest latticework done with nail-less joinery and groove systems. The lattice window allows light to filter into the interior of the prayer hall.

Far left
Walnut wood carving, Srinagar, Kashmir

A master craftsman works on a low table, as woodcarving is usually done while sitting on the floor with the comforts of the *kangri* and the *hukka*.

Centre
Detail of walnut jewel box, contemporary, Kashmir

Elaborate relief work and deeply carved floral jewel box tops exhibit the forms of the rose, iris and lotus with a bee nestling amidst them. They are not mere naturalistic expressions but are devised, stylised and interpreted by the craftsman.

Walnut jewel box, contemporary, Kashmir

Craftsmen carving box lids are a common sight in every contemporary *karkhana*. Various kinds of chisels used to obtain different textures are devised through indigenous knowledge and skill.

Hand-driven lathe, Anantnag, Kashmir

A typical hand-lathe is driven by a string-and-bow. Generally, two people — one for driving the lathe and the other for chiselling the object — are required. Such lathe-made objects are polished and coloured by turning the lathe while applying the finishing material.

Far right

Woodcraft shop, Anantnag, Kashmir

Traditional folk woodcraft items include ladles, *chonchas*, of various sizes; the rice-measure, *longura*; plain and decorated wooden sandals, *kharav*; the spinning wheel, *yender*; childrens' toys and child-walkers.

The use of colourful lacquer and foil paste is a typical feature that highlights the technique of filling in the carved motifs in bridal sandals with hot lacquer colours and applying white metal paint over the toys, child-walkers and spinning wheels. The white-metal paint is made from tin foil, *kalai*, which is beaten on a stone slab with a wooden beater and mixed with some drops of liquid glue till the metal turns into paste.

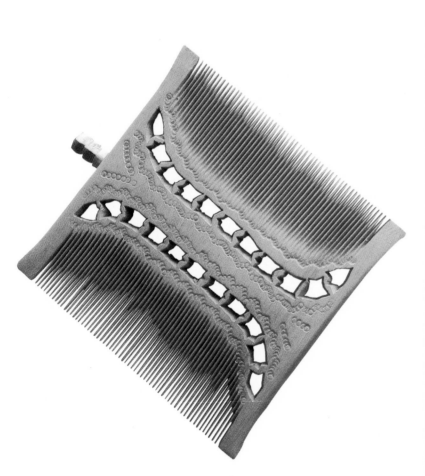

the southern parts of the valley, are typical products of the region. Generally, craftsmen produce items on hand-driven lathes, but earlier hand-carved rice ladles, rice measures and bridal sandals represented the typical folk craft of the area. Now, many new products including toys, spinning wheels and cradles have been added to the range. It is the wood of the willow tree (*Salix tetrasperma*) and horse chestnut tree (*Aesculus indica*), known as *vir* and *han* in Kashmiri, which provides the raw material for Anantnag carving work. The most intriguing feature of this work is the way, for instance, in which unbroken rings of woods are carved out of the outer circumference of the handle of a long, wooden spoon. Through skillful turning on the hand lathe, a series of such bracelet-like rings can move freely up and down the base rod and are prevented from falling off or slipping down by the outward swell of the base rod at strategic places. It takes very skillful handling of the lathe to make these rings. In India, such work is peculiar to Kashmir though it has a parallel in Mexican woodcraft. Anantnag carvings are usually very brightly coloured — deep pink, orange and green being the colours used most often. Sometimes they are also given a glittering surface by rubbing a shiny chemical after sand papering.

An unusual type of wood is obtained from the *chikri* tree (*Buxux semperuirens*) which grows abundantly in the southern slopes of the Pir Panjal in Rajouri district in Jammu. The *chikri* tree thrives at an altitude of 1,800 to 2,100 metres above sea level. In appearance it is an ordinary tree, attaining a maximum height of 6.1 m with a trunk of 15 to 25 cms in diameter. It is only when the trunk is cut in cross-section to reveal its completely non-fibrous, non-porous wood, that one notices its unique qualities. *Chikri* wood is a light honey colour and has hardly any grain.

Trade in *chikri* wood products is centuries old and items made in Jammu were supplied not only in villages on the slopes of the Pir Panjal, but also to localities stretching from Badgam to the Shupyan and Kulgam areas of the Kashmir valley. *Chikri* wood products were sold by peddlers who wandered from village to village and were also available at famous shrines like Reshimol in Anantnag, in the shrines of Achipal and Pakharpora village and at Nund Rishi at Chirar-e-Sharif.

The oldest and most well-known *chikri* wood item

is the traditional, double-sided comb or *kangi*. These combs have extremely fine teeth and are often decorated with intricate *jali* work. They are especially popular among women of the Gujjar and Bakarwal tribes, but are also used by other village women of Jammu and Kashmir. The Kashmiri *kangi* was also a great favourite of Mughal princesses. In fact, the cluster of villages known as Thana Mandi, which remains the main centre for *chikri* woodcrafts, is situated on the main Mughal route to Kashmir. The Mughals would halt there before beginning the climb up the Panjal peaks which led to the Kashmir valley. And Mughal patronage played an important role in making Thana Mandi a centre for the crafts of Jammu.

Today, about 30 *chikri* wood carvers remain in Thana Mandi and the demand for their craft has survived the onslaught of cheap, factory-made plastic products. Approximately, 1,000 *chikri kangis* are manufactured each month and are despatched by the craftsmen of Thana Mandi. These craftsmen have taken steps to protect their craft from extinction by forming a co-operative society and the product range has also been widened to include jewellery boxes, ashtrays, ordinary combs and cups and saucers.

The most prevalent forms of woodwork in Ladakh are to be found in the Buddhist monasteries. The earliest Buddhist buildings were *vassavasas*, temporary shelters from the rain, where monks retreated only during the monsoon. These later gave way to brick structures called *avasa* or *arama*. As the concept of the monastery grew and wealthy patrons began to finance construction work, stone buildings which were inhabited by monks all the year round, began to come up. It is only these, the *lenas* of stone and rock built from A.D. 1000 onwards which survive intact today. In them we find ample evidence of the woodcarving skills of the people of Ladakh.

There is a theory that woodworkers from Kashmir may also have worked at the sites of the great monasteries of Ladakh which display strong Kashmiri-style elements in the carving. This style is, in fact, strikingly prevalent throughout the architectural decorations of the western Himalayas.

Certainly, at various stages of history, the arts of the Himalayas were influenced by those of many of the ruling kingdoms of India. For the Buddhist monasteries, which were centres of art, education and

Far left

Chikri woodcraft, Thana Mandi, Rajouri district, Jammu

The most popular *chikri* wood item is the comb, *kangi*, made by women. The *kangis* are decorated with delicate, lattice-like patterns and the creamy softness of the wood enhances its likeness to ivory. The *kangi* holds oil which is automatically released on to the strands of hair while combing.

Comb of chikri wood being made in Thana Mandi, Poonch

A simple lathe is operated by hand while the foot holds it in place. This is all that is required to mould the soft creamy-textured wood into a fine-toothed comb with carved decorations.

religious instruction, were situated in isolated sections of the major trade routes connecting Tibet to India. Travellers and religious seekers often carried sculptures, paintings or literary and religious texts with them. Through these encounters the artists of the Himalayas absorbed motifs and styles from the Kushan (50 B.C.- A.D. 210) and other empires. In addition to these, Sassanian, Khotanese and Uighur influences are seen in western Himalayan woodcarving.

Timber was used in various places to construct Buddhist temples and monasteries and the most striking wooden elements in the building were the pillars which supported the ceiling. The length of the main shaft of the column was determined by the length of timber available to the monks. Yet, as the monastery structures became more complex, the desire to increase the height of the ceiling led to a clever architectural solution. The column was normally placed on a separate wooden base and the capital rested on top of the main shaft. To increase height, the capital was doubled, or even tripled, as described in Legshay Thubten Gyatsho's *Gateway to the Temple*. "Atop the lintel (main beam) is a plant called nagaline and atop that two levels of woodwork consisting of the lotus and dharma stick. Ordinary temples may be decorated with twelve levels of fine architectural woodwork or should a cathedral be extremely great and elaborate, it may be beautified in the above forementioned *(sic)* way but with a total of sixteen to eighteen tiers of architectural detail".

The columns were intricately carved and the most common motif for the main part of the pillar was the lotus, with its petals opening outwards. The capital could be variously embellished with the head of a water demon, *makara*, a lotus or a *mantra*.

The complex of buildings called *Alchi-chos-khor*, the religious enclave of Alchi village in Ladakh, contains some of the finest examples of western Himalayan woodcarving. In a courtyard leading to the central temple, Du-khang, is a carved wooden stupa, exactly like those depicted in the Alchi wall murals. A suspended arch over the doorway to the temple has a series of lion-like animals and five seated Buddhas are carved on the doorway. These are surrounded by gods and goddesses from the Buddhist pantheon and the carving is further elaborated with flower, bird and animal motifs.

Far left
Wooden carvings at Alchi, Ladakh

During the reign of Lhachen Takpa and Lhachen Changchub, Semspa kings of Ladakh, the great translator Rinchen Zangpo visited Ladakh and founded the famous shrine of Alchi in A.D. 1020-1035. Numerous artists from Kashmir and Tibet were invited to participate in building the shrine.

After Lalitaditya and Shankaravarman, the Kashmiri style of woodwork and wall-painting continued to flourish and travelled along the famous trade route of Central Asia to enrich the monastery of Alchi.

The wall brackets are suspended at the entrance of the first shrine and support a small balcony.

Lathe-turned butter bowl, Ladakh

Lathe-turning is a late introduction in Ladakhi woodwork. The technique is very rare in the region, since joinery and hand-carving are used to make low eating and study tables which are then decorated with painted patterns. The bowl is unconventional in the sense that the motifs employed are borrowed from Kashmiri painters. The repetition of tree motifs is a typical feature of Kashmiri decoration.

In the *Sum-Tasek*, the three-tiered temple of Alchi, beams of wood protruding through the walls have been carved into lions' heads. Carved images of the Buddha are also set between short, supporting columns.

Apart from its use in these columns, wood was decoratively used on balconies, particularly if the parapet had a wooden frame. Timber was often utilised as a surface on the ground floor, since the monks had limited tools at their disposal to level the mountainous terrain. Wood was also employed in the roof structure, as can be seen in the Ri-dzong monastery. Here Lombardi poplar columns form the superstructure of the roof while several layers of willow branches form a mesh which has been plastered over with fine clay.

Besides architectural woodwork, Ladakh also has a tradition of carved and painted furniture. The *choktsey*, a low table with elaborate carving on four sides, is a typical example. Larger tables and cupboards as well as bowls used for Buddhist rituals are also made. All woodwork in Ladakh is painted in fairly bright colours obtained from various natural sources. The local plant, *tsot*, is used to make maroon and the bark of the apricot tree for yellow.

The abundant mountain trees of Jammu, Kashmir and Ladakh, silent and giving, have certainly been a boon to craftsmen, stimulating the woodworker's imagination and providing him with material for hundreds of years. The earth's resources, however, cannot last forever, and already many of the trees used for Kashmiri woodcrafts have become protected species. Both walnut and *chikri* are available only to craftsmen within Kashmir on a limited scale and the sale of walnut wood outside the state is banned. Hopefully such measures, if adequately carried out, will help to preserve the natural balance of a beautiful region, as well as save one of the finest craft forms of India from becoming a colourful legend of the past.

Architectural interior, Ladakh

The carved gables and cornices which are superimposed with coloured decorations are special features of the architecture. Even the carved motifs are painted with temperas and then lacquered over.

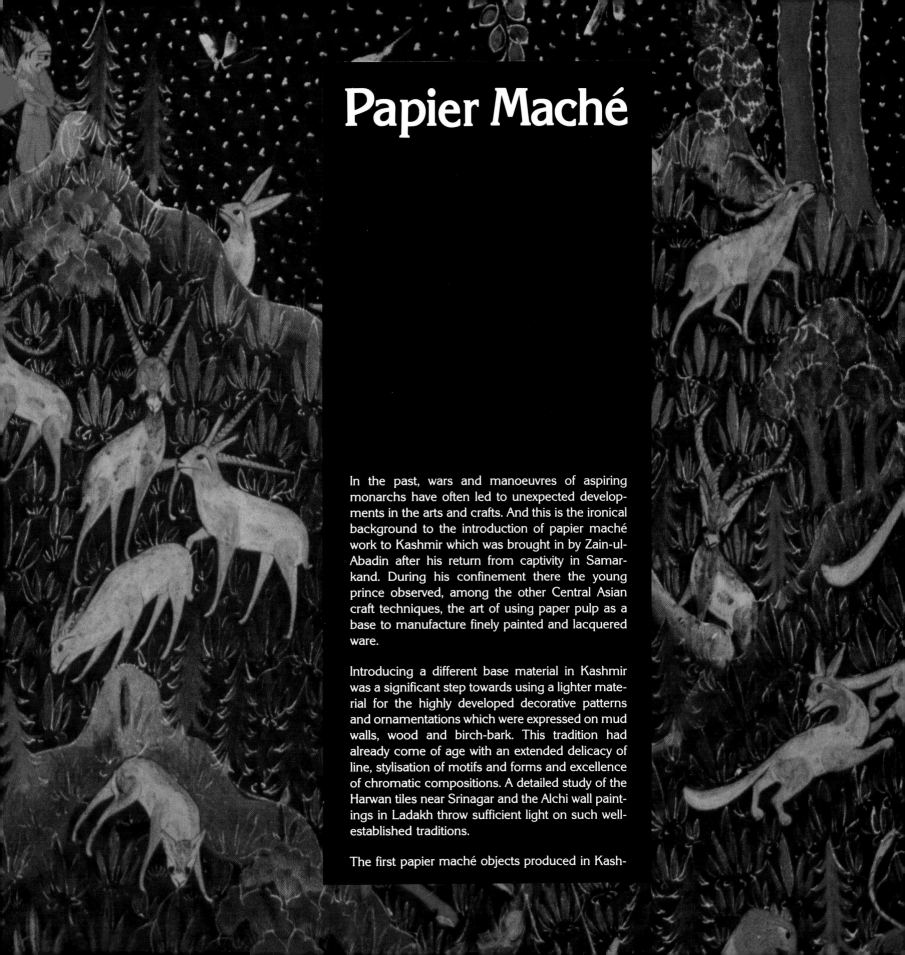

Papier Maché

In the past, wars and manoeuvres of aspiring monarchs have often led to unexpected developments in the arts and crafts. And this is the ironical background to the introduction of papier maché work to Kashmir which was brought in by Zain-ul-Abadin after his return from captivity in Samarkand. During his confinement there the young prince observed, among the other Central Asian craft techniques, the art of using paper pulp as a base to manufacture finely painted and lacquered ware.

Introducing a different base material in Kashmir was a significant step towards using a lighter material for the highly developed decorative patterns and ornamentations which were expressed on mud walls, wood and birch-bark. This tradition had already come of age with an extended delicacy of line, stylisation of motifs and forms and excellence of chromatic compositions. A detailed study of the Harwan tiles near Srinagar and the Alchi wall paintings in Ladakh throw sufficient light on such well-established traditions.

The first papier maché objects produced in Kash-

mir were *kalamdans*, long horizontal cases for holding pens, brushes and ink-pots, giving it the original local name of the craft, *kar-i-kalamdani*, pen-case work. Over time, the repertoire of articles grew and by the Mughal period in Kashmir history (1586-1782), included bedsteads, doors, window frames and panels for walls and ceilings. It is also said that most of the palanquins used in Mughal courts were specially brought from Kashmir. The Mughals seem to have been great enthusiasts for papier maché work, often commissioning entire communities of craftsmen to make gifts as well as decorative items for their palaces.

Between 1589 and 1666, the first European travellers entered the Kashmir valley and on returning to their homelands spread the word about the unusual craft they had seen in India. The demand for papier maché products grew and commercial agents from Europe began suggesting items which would be popular with their clientele. Apparently, the nest of boxes, vases and *soorai* or water container forms first began to be manufactured at the suggestion of French shawl agents who also sent shawls to France in papier maché boxes. These boxes were sold separately and were expensive, highly coveted items. It is probably at this stage that the western world began to know this craft form by its French name — 'papier maché'.

By the 20th century the market for more traditional items such as *kalamdans* and palanquins had waned and in his study of the arts and crafts of Kashmir in 1912, the historian A. Mitra records that papier maché work had deteriorated in quality. By this time, papier maché was being used to make souvenirs and small, more easily produced objects to meet the demand for less expensive examples of the craft. Items like picture frames, screens, tables, tea caddies, trays and candlesticks were now commonly available.

The debate on the updating of traditional crafts to suit modern markets is a long and tricky one and cannot be gone into here, but it is important to remember that alongside the overtly commercial and often shoddily produced papier maché work flooding gift shops in India and abroad, there still remain highly skilled craftsmen who painstakingly produce work of uncompromising quality. Among such craftsmen aesthetic sensibilities and hereditary skills govern the manufacture of any article they choose, be it a *kalamdan* or a coffee table.

Previous page

Detail of round tray; contemporary; Srinagar, Kashmir

Shikargah, a hunting scene which celebrates the richness of nature, is a well-known pattern used in carpets, embroidery and wood carving. Papier maché painting allows for fine detailing, evident in the depiction of moths, butterflies and a variety of plants in this tray.

***Kalamdan*, pen case; 22.5 cms × 10.2 cms × 10.2 cms; 20th century; Sri Pratap Singh Museum; Srinagar**

The non-oily variety of pine wood *kayur* (*Pinus excelsa*) is ideally suited for painting over and does not cause blisters and other surface problems.

The pattern, a direct copy from the famous Kashmiri *kani* shawl, is a late introduction into the craft. Even now the pattern does not find a proper place in the vocabulary of traditional papier maché patterns and is referred to as *shawl tarah*, the shawl pattern. Indigenous mineral and vegetable colours have been used in this *kalamdan*.

The techniques involved in papier maché production are divided into two distinct categories. The first is *sakhtasazi*, making the object, the second is *naqashi*, painting the surface.

To prepare a form the *sakhta-saz* grinds paper, cloth, rice straw and copper sulphate into a pulp which is moulded around a base shape. At first, papier maché craftsmen made their own clay moulds but today they use wooden or metal moulds made by other craftsmen. After the pulp has dried and hardened to the required shape, it is carefully cut from the mould with a fine saw. The two halves are then joined together again with glue and the surface is evened with an iron file called *kathwav*.

The form is then covered with a thick, white solution made from gypsum and glue. In the past, gypsum was often obtained from the stuccos of old, deserted buildings. When this white layer is dry it is rubbed smooth with a chunk of over-baked red clay called *kurkot*, which has also been rubbed and made even. Small pieces of fine tissue paper are then pasted on the form in layers to prevent cracks from forming in the gypsum coat. The object is rubbed and smoothened a final time, to produce a very finely burnished surface. It then becomes ready to receive the ground coat of colour.

Some papier maché objects are made in wood and these fall in a separate category from pure paper-pulp objects. These items save time and labour and are made into cheap souvenirs. Generally, they are made from the light timber of the *kayur* variety of a forest pine (*Pinus excelsa*).

In an older form of wood-based papier-maché work, the shape was covered with a stretched layer of thin sheepskin, which provided a more subtle and smooth surface than paper and took colouring pigments well.

Traditional colours for the ground layer are gold, white, black, red and blue. Many contemporary papier maché craftsmen use commercial distemper colours but the traditional art of manufacturing colours is still followed by some.

The *naqash*, the artist or pattern drawer, and his assistants prepared the colours for painting the papier maché objects, a long and laborious process. Pigments in stone or clot form were tied in a bag, moistened with water and beaten thoroughly.

Section of book cover; 26.2 cms × 14.7 cms; late 18th century; School of Designs Museum; Srinagar

The basic form is prepared through a special process used for items like book covers, plates for book illustrations and miniature paintings. Many sheets of hand-made paper are pasted one upon another in the requisite thickness. A fine muslin sheet which serves as a binder and as protection against warping and cracking is then pasted over them. For better results, the muslin is placed alternately with the sheets of paper. The binding agent is thick starch prepared from rice-flour mixed with a little copper sulphate.

The main body of the cover is an important example of a pattern that is generally used to cover an entire surface. Its unit can be repeated and manoeuvred in all directions in order to cover any requisite space. The main body, when filled, is called *mattan*, the pattern employed is *gonder*, the tuft, and the main border contains a running pattern of *yember-zal*, narcissus florals.

The patterning in the main body of this book cover is one of the finest examples of linear brush work and is an ideal balance between floral and linear forms. The medium used is liquid gold.

Far left

Detail of vanity box lid; School of Designs Museum, Srinagar

The central medallion of this lid is a historically important one. This ancient design was considered extremely auspicious by the *yogis* and *sadaks* of the Shakt and Tantra systems whose philosophy and spiritual practices were deeply-rooted in pre-Buddhist Kashmir, and were responsible for strengthening the Mahayana system of Buddhism. The design points towards a famous stage in *sri-chakra*, the graphic symbolisation of meditation, or *sadhana*. Graphically, this stage of *sadhana* is depicted through an *ashta-dala-padma* an eight-petalled lotus, enclosed in a *mandala*, circle, or three circles. This graphic expression is prominent in Dakshinakali Yantra and in the Buddhist art of the Harwan school.

On this lid-top, the eight-petalled form is filled with eight branches of florals projecting from the central point or *bindoo*. The *bindoo* is replaced by a typical floral form which finds its first expression in the Harwan school of Srinagar.

Cylindrical vanity or toilet box with lid, wood-based, papier maché, hand lathe product; height: 18.5 cms, dia. 14 cms, top dia. 13.4 cms; 18th century; School of Designs Museum; Srinagar, Kashmir

The Kashmiri *sanzi-war* or vanity box, made to contain traditional accessories for make-up, owes its origin to *saz*, meaning to prepare and *war*, from *vaar* which is derived from *vihar*, resting or residing place.

A thin coating of gypsum and glue is overlaid on the wooden object and a final coating of red-lead provides the ground for decoration. The freshness of the colour indicates the purity of the mineral dyes and their indigenous methods of preparation. The colour blue is an extraction of Indican (indigo lead). The distribution around the body of an ancient tree motif from the Harwan School sobers the intensity of the almost fluorescent colours. The direct brush strokes used to evolve a motif indicate a deftness of expression.

Far left, top

Preparation of pulp

Waste paper, thoroughly soaked, is pounded in an *okhli*, an indigenously carved stone mortar with a hand-made wooden pestle. The pulp is not reduced to a fine paste, but is left in a semi-coarse condition. The pounded material is mixed with a rice-flour paste containing a small portion of copper sulphate, *neela-thotha*, which is an effective insecticide.

When paper was not manufactured by machine and printing techniques were unknown, manuscripts were highly prized as references for history and tradition. Thus, waste paper was not easily available and cotton and jute rags were mixed with waste paper.

Centre and right

Application of *astar*, an insulation, and preparation of the mould

A craftsman cuts sections of waste paper to put a detachable lining on the mould in order to insulate it from the pulp. Strips of paper of required sizes are arranged over the mould surface and attached to vital points with minor specks of paste. The craftsmen places the pulp over the insulated mould very carefully as the lining should not be displaced and most of the work, especially at the crucial corners, curves and extremities is done by hand. At times, to achieve perfection and accuracy, the final shaping is done with the help of the *nala*, or spatula, which resembles a painting knife.

Far left, bottom

Sakhtasazi preparing the basic form in a typical _karkhana_, Srinagar, Kashmir

Sakhtasazi is derived from *sakth* (Persian for "basic") and *sazi*, the act of forming or evolving. The popular name for the craft is *chot*, meaning the plain and white. *Chot-wol* or *sakhta-saz* is the maker of the plain object.

A *sakhtsazi karkhana* is generally owned by an individual craft worker and forms a part of his household. Occasionally the head of the family engages daily workers from smaller households to work in the *karkhana* or in their own homes. When household space is short, rooms in the locality are rented.

Here, one *chot-wol* lays the pulp with a spatula while the other smoothens an uneven edge with a rough iron file or *kathav*.

Bottom, far right

Naqashi studio, Srinagar, Kashmir

The *naqashi* studio, converted from one of the rooms in the house is peaceful and quiet, compared to the *sakhtasazi karkhana*. Here, seated on a *waggu* mat, craftsmen prepare the surface of small boxes for painting.

Master craftsman at work on the gold-leaf technique

In applying gold leaf the brush-work patterning is done with a solution of animal glue mixed with crystal-sugar. The master craftsman maintains a smooth brush flow by keeping the solution warm over live embers in an indigenous terracotta container called *manah*. The painted areas remain sticky and thus retain the gold leaf.

Far right

Jewellery box; oblong; hectagonal; 26.8 cms × 16.6 cms × 19.8 cms; mid-20th century; School of Designs Museum; Srinagar

This jewellery box is a typical example of the beginnings of change from traditional style and content. The base material is pine wood. A change is visible in treatment of material, style and content. The treatment has become timid and baroque. A mild sense of perspective is a result of the western influence that crept into Pahari schools in general but in papier maché particularly due to the practice of copying prints of old paintings and illustrations. The illustration on this box is one such example. Local craftsmen had no knowledge of human anatomy. Modern commercial paints have been used and the gold at the border of the lid is artificial. The calligraphy does not bear any relation to the theme and content of the painting on the box.

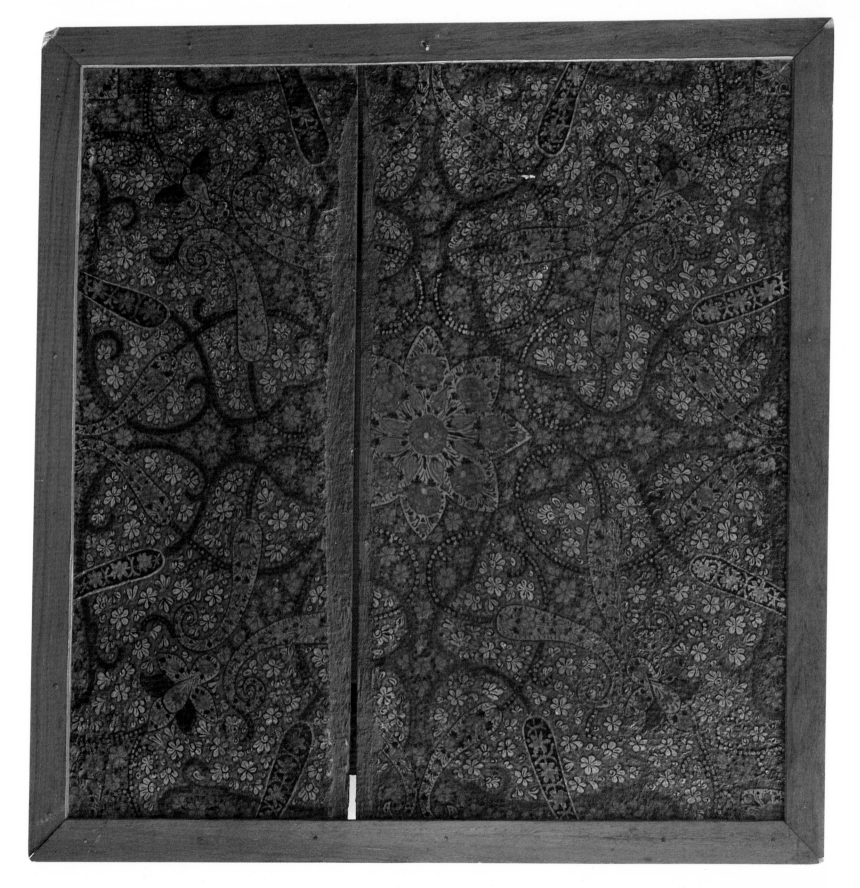

They were then ground into paste on a stone slab and dried into a powder on a charcoal fire after which the powder was mixed with an amber varnish and immersed in water. This solution was vigorously stirred and slowly poured into a clean vessel. After the colour had settled, the clear water would be poured out.

The pigments were of both vegetable and mineral origin and the raw materials came from local as well as foreign sources. White lead came from Russia and body white was prepared from a local stone called *shalla-noon* or *bus-watter* in Kashmiri. The source for clay deposits was near Manasbal Lake and verdigris (green), a mineral product, came from Surat, in Gujarat. Lapis lazuli, brought from Yarkand across the Karakoram range, was used for ultramarine. Other blues were extracted from *wood*, a genus of cruciferous plants mostly found around the Mediterranean. Another shade of dark blue and violet was extracted from indigo, a tropical plant belonging to the species of *Indigofera*. Browns and siennas were made from a clay imported from Armenia. Zarnik, a kind of yellow stone, was the raw material for yellow, while other shades of brilliant yellow were produced from the flower *gule-kysu* and a wild plant, *woftangil*, both found in Kashmir. Fine quality yellows were extracted from saffron, which grew in abundance in Kashmir. Oranges were made from *Carthamus*, a sunflower plant or a thistle-like composite cultivated in India. Various shades of red were derived from cochineal, a local forest wood called Lin and a tropical American and Mediterranean tree with red heartwood called Logwood from the botanical family *Caesalpinia*, locally known as *lod*. From dried and green walnut skins, light browns were obtained. Various types of black were produced from iron filings and pomegranate skins, the latter also being used to make light browns. Black for details and pattern work was prepared from lampblack, while black for large areas and plain groundwork was made from semi-burnt, fumigated cowdung.

Papier maché objects with real silver or gold leaf decorations or with a gold background on which patterns are painted in other colours, are particularly interesting as they display yet another skill of the *naqashi* and indicate the interdependence and cooperation between the craftsmen and the valley.

A community of gold beaters lives in the centre of

Ceiling piece; late 19th century; Old Secretariat; Srinagar, Kashmir

The *shawl-tarah*, a late introduction in papier maché art patterns, derived from the famous Kashmiri shawl. The linear formations juxtaposed with floral decoration are rendered in a cohesive manner to enhance the brocade-like effect. When the Old Secretariat building, which was adorned with this beautiful ceiling, was destroyed in a fire a decade ago, parts of the ceiling, including this piece, were retrieved.

the ancient city of Srinagar and produces the fine leaves of precious metal which are used to decorate the various crafts of the region. Gold leaf is applied to papier maché objects by first painting the desired pattern in a light colour with a liquid mix of glue and sugar. While the mixture is still sticky because of the sugar content the metal leaf is applied and adheres only to the portions painted with the mixture. For liquid gold or silver paint, the leaf is mashed with the fingers in glue, salt and water, until it completely dissolves. The mixture is then allowed to settle, after which the gold paste is applied with a fine brush. Gold work is burnished with an agate stone.

The designs used in papier maché *naqashi* are very intricate and their application requires a great deal of skill and accuracy. The patterns are painted free hand. The *naqash* draws from the reservoir of patterns and motifs in his memory. The chosen design is first outlined in a light colour and the spaces outlining flowers or other forms which are to be filled with colour are initially painted white. After this, the flowers, birds and other motifs are painted. Details in black outline or other dark colours are painted in later. The gold leaf is applied first and then detailed over, while the details in liquid gold are done last. Finally, a coat of lacquer made of linseed oil and pine resin is applied. The brushes used for *naqashi* were formerly made of cats' hair, while today commercially manufactured brushes are used.

Motifs such as the lotus and iris, *sosan*; water lily, *gule-neelofar*; narcissus, *nargis*; field crocus, *nyov*; and flying geese, comprise the essential vocabulary of papier maché decorations. Very often, patterns found in woven shawls such as the Tree of Life, *kalpa-vriksha*, and the *chinar* leaf motif, derived from the Booni, a type of plane tree, *Platanus orientalis*, were also used. Important later additions are the rose and apple blossoms. The composition of these two motifs gave birth to the famous *gule-vilayat* design.

Non-figurative patterns are divided into several categories. Often they are enclosed within a border, *daurdar*. The pattern can form a circle, making it *chand-dar* or full-moon. If the pattern divides into four quarter-moon shapes, it is referred to as *chand-chautahi*, or quarter moons. In the case of the *mehrab*, the pattern forms an arch. Another famous design, *hazara*, was made up of all the

Jewellery chest; contemporary; Srinagar, Kashmir

Western influence is evident in the Victorian form of this jewel box. The typically traditional *chinar* pattern is highlighted against a dark background, rendering a jewel-like effect. The kingfisher, golden oriole and the Kashmir valley's favourite *bulbul* are popular figures in papier maché painting, and reflect the influence of nature on the craftspeople. The painting is executed in the embossed technique where the pattern is raised with a thick solution of gypsum and glue, applied with a brush.

motifs used in papier maché work and this design along with the *gul-andar-gul* is considered to represent the spirit and grandeur of the craft.

Exposure to European painting resulted in some changes in the traditional motifs and patterns. Many craftsmen, intrigued by the "realism" of academic painting, tried to introduce naturalistic elements in their *naqashi*. The ensuing mixture of styles has rarely been successful. The efforts to show light and shadow and three-dimensional forms seem like clumsy intruders in a world of lively, vibrant lines and clear, rich colours which need no artificial rules of perspective to measure the depth of the craftsmen's skills. The traditional patterns and designs bear witness to the artisan's affinity with nature and his awe and admiration for the abundance of colour and forms found in his own environment.

Far left

Ornamental bowl; contemporary; Srinagar; Kashmir

The shape of the bowl has been taken from a typical Kashmiri eating bowl, popularly known as *bushkab*. Although the shape is a traditional one, the decoration is a copy of an old painting — reflecting a mixture of the Rajput style with western influences. The European elements are visible in the effort to mould human forms and in the introduction of perspective, visible in the arrangement of the figures and the dishes of the feast. The colours employed are modern commercial paints.

***Naqashi karkhana*, Srinagar, Kashmir**

Contemporary *karkhanas* have proliferated because of increased commercial activity and have now come out of the household environment. In such *karkhanas* many *shagirds*, apprentices, are seen at work, presided over by an *ustad* or master craftsman.

The typical colourful patterning is seen being done by both the *ustad* and the *shagirds*. The *ustad* is usually held in high esteem by the *shagirds*. A typical gesture of respect is expressed in the preparation of the *chillum* for the *hukka*.

Nomadic Crafts

"To protect, forsooth, the Nagas, who came to seek shelter afraid of Garuda, it stretches out its arms high above in the guise of mountain walls", wrote Kalhana, the 12th century Kashmiri historian, referring to the mountains enveloping Kashmir. The famous Chinese traveller Hwan Thsang also made note of the formidable mountains. While the Kashmiri peasant kept his distance from the mountains and ended his cultivation where the alluvial soil of the valley ended, that is, "where the maple, the poplar and the willow do not grow", the nomadic Gujjar and Bakarwal tribes make this area their temporary yet regular home.

In the early summer months a traveller to Kashmir on the National Highway, still called the B.C. (Banihal Cart) Road, will pass, every now and then, small *dheras* or caravans of mountain people.

These are the nomads of Kashmir, the Gujjars and Bakarwals, who set out every year from the winter pastures to the high mountain *behaks* or meadows that border the glaciers deep in the interior of the Himalayas. A closer view reveals that entire households — with their pots and pans, small sailing cloth tents, an assortment of blankets, sacks of maize flour and other essential goods — are on the move on their pack-horses. A small kid with a broken leg which cannot make it with the flock or a few fowls that will add meat, and variety, to their otherwise essentially vegetarian and frugal diet may be tied over these packs. An infirm man or sick woman with a child tied to her back may be astride another horse, but the rest of the family — men and women and children walk the entire distance to the predetermined night camp-site. Following this caravan are flocks of sheep and goats herded by a few tall, bearded men and accompanied by a fierce-looking watch dog.

This transhumance or movement of entire families and their flocks is not an unrestricted and un-directed wandering but is a mode of living and means of sustenance for these communities. The routes they have followed over the years are now recognised as "corridors" of social links between them, the settled farmers and other grazing com-munities. Year after year, with a minimum of facili-ties, these nomads move with their flocks and fami-lies traversing a difficult terrain of narrow gorges, slippery mountain paths and rocky slopes. Fre-quently, particularly on the higher reaches and mountain passes, they are trapped in blizzards and storms.

The nomads and their flocks spend the winter months from November to March in the hills of Riasi, Poonch and Rajouri and the areas surround-ing the foothills of Jammu. They begin their sea-sonal migration towards the summer pastures around the first week of April and converge along seven different routes depending on the entry points or mountain passes in the Pir Panjal range, the paths followed in the valley and their eventual passage through the Himalayan range. On each route, they cover an average distance of 300 kilometres each way, with stopovers at different stages on their upward journey, till they reach the alpine pastures. They remain here for three or four months and return by the same routes only when the climate becomes too cold and conditions too inhospitable for them and their flocks.

The earliest historical reference to the Gujjars as a distinct community is found in the *Harsha Charita* of Bāna Bhat, the poet, who writes of them in the seventh century as "huns". The derivation of "juzr" or "khazer" of the Arab historians and the "gheyser" of the Jews are known to be identical with the Gujjars.

Previous page

Embroidered *chhat* or saddlebag, Pahalgam, Kashmir

A detail of decorations done by Bakarwal women on a *chhat* or sack made from goat's hair. A combination of stem stitch, chain stitch and hemstitch in woollen thread is ornamented with tiny brass bells and woollen pompoms. Their saddlebags contain clothes and blankets and are tied to the backs of ponies during their journeys. The motifs and design of each strip indicate an attempt at imitating in embroidery the woven *zanzeer* de-signs of blanket borders. Diamond and triangular shapes in brilliant pinks, reds, yel-lows, oranges and blues achieve the effect of a woven border more quickly than if these de-signs were to be woven on the *kani* loom.

Bakarwal *dhera* on the move, Kashmir

A nomadic family with a pack train of horses precedes its flock in search of greener pas-tures. In their annual seasonal move, the nomads trek through rugged mountain terrain ending in the treeless alpine grasslands called *behaks* in the inner Himalayas. There they spend the summer months before moving back to the warmer areas of the Jammu re-gion to spend the winter.

Kunhari Gujjars, Sonamarg, Kashmir

Gujjars camp by the roadside near Sonamarg which leads to Kargil through the Zoji *La* or pass. The old woman and child wear caps typical of the Kunhari group of Gujjars and Bakarwals. These caps have a longer flap with a straight edging at the back and combine embroidery with patchwork. The style of shirt is again worn only by Kunhari women and consists of black cloth ornamented with some embroidery or coloured patches. The Kunhar-is are closest to the original tribes descending from the Greco-Indians and are interrelated with the Gujjars of Gujarat and the tribes settled around Gujjaranwal in Pakistan.

Far right

Old Bakarwal with his pack horses, Pahalgam, Kashmir

An old Bakarwal readies his pack horse before he moves to the next camp. The rope netting called *trandgi* is used to keep the load in place. The rope around the neck is called *seeli* and the *nukta* or harness straps are made with goat's hair by the men and sometimes decorated with bells and multi-coloured pompoms. The pink and orange blankets atop the pony are woven by local weavers with coloured yarn dyed and given to them by the Bakarwals. *Lois* or blankets from Sopore or Bandipur form the base of the pack.

The Gujjars of Kashmir are said to be part of a larger tribe which dispersed over Afghanistan, Iran, India, Pakistan and parts of Central Asia. It is believed that their influx into Kashmir came through two separate waves of migration. The first and direct one was from the Gurjara tribe of Rajputana, Gujarat and Kathiawar, after a serious outbreak of famine in those regions. Some of the migrating tribes are thought to have moved to the Punjab in Northern India while others went further north to areas including Kagan, Swat, Hazara, Kashmir and Gilgit. A sub-sect of the Gujjars, the Kunhari Gujjars with their black shirts and distinctive caps have maintained a style of dress closest to that of the original tribes descending from the Greco-Indians, and the Allaiwal Bakarwals, who originally came from the Allai area of Hazara, in Pakistan, have further moved into Kashmir. Each group, in fact, retains vestiges of dress and jewellery linking them to their earlier associations.

The second and later wave of migration during the last century came from the North Indian plains where the Gujjars were allowed to acquire land after the irrigation of the former thorn steppes of Punjab deprived them of winter pastures. They settled in permanent holdings in the winter and continued their seasonal migration in summer. Most Gujjars are, therefore, semi-settled farmers. They erected their winter settlements above the outer edges of lands belonging to the Kashmiri rice farmers and on the higher slopes of side valleys.

Depending upon their subsistence pattern and the degree of transhumance, over the years the Gujjars have evolved into different sections. The main group who were the early settlers are the valley Gujjars, whose livelihood depends primarily on cows and buffaloes and who sell butter and fresh cheese. They own unirrigated land and grow maize which is their staple food. In the summer most family members move with their cattle to the higher pastures where they have grazing rights.

The Banihara or Dudhi Gujjars, who are buffalo breeders, represent the second group. Their principal means of livelihood is the sale of buffalo milk and milk products. Formerly, most Banihara families used to move to Punjab in winter but with increasingly modern and intensive agriculture being practised in Punjab today, it has become harder for them to spend the winter there. Many of them, therefore, have become sedentary, acquiring land and remaining near city centres like Jammu and Kathua. Some Baniharas continue to go to their summer pastures in Bhaderwah and Kishtwar while others have sought pastures beyond the Pir Panjal range in the valley.

The third group, the Bakarwals or goatherds, are believed by scholars to have come from different ethnic stock. They invaded Kashmir about a century ago in order to retain their nomadic life against forced settlements in their original habitat around the Kagan valley.

The Bakarwals lead a totally nomadic life and their economy is concentrated on huge flocks of Kagan goats and, more recently, some sheep. They support themselves through the sale of goat products such as meat, hair and skin. Some of the hair is retained to make pack lashings, lengths of webbing, ropes and rope net bags.

Though they enter into trade and economic relationships with the settled population both in the Jammu region and in the Kashmir valley, over the centuries the Gujjars and Bakarwals have maintained their special identity, customs and social structures. Even when they establish semi-permanent structures and settlements they do not intrude upon the rice, wheat or sugarcane fields of the settled farmers, preferring to live apart on higher lands. The temperate and alpine grasses supporting the transhumant pastoral economy of the Gujjars and Bakarwals, like that of the Kirghiz in the Tien Shan, is an interesting social phenomenon. They live in small, flat-roofed *kothas* made of logs and mud. These dark, windowless structures have a partition that separates the people from their herds and usually families sit round their hearths from which smoke billows constantly. The *kothas* are widely dispersed over the hillsides where maize is cultivated virtually upto the doorsteps and when the maize is ripening, the Gujjars arm themselves with drums and tin cans and keep up a fearful din to frighten off bears.

The Bakarwals who are fully nomadic live in tents for most of their lives. Lately, however, the more wealthy have begun acquiring land and building houses in their winter grazing areas, sometimes encroaching on forest land.

As a race the Gujjars and Bakarwals are distinguished by their tall, thin figures and sharp, acquiline

Banihara Gujjar family in a temporary shed, Kakhyal, Kathua

A Banihara Gujjar husband and wife in a semi-permanent dwelling. The family cooks and dwells at one end while the other end is used as a stable. Baniharas are Gujjars who have taken to rearing buffaloes and selling milk, cheese and clarified butter in the towns of Jammu and Kathua.

The man wears a long shirt, a *lungi* or cloth which he wraps around his waist, a waistcoat and a turban. His beard is trimmed close to his face, the result of interaction with city people. The woman has the traditional embroidered *kurta* or shirt, and leather shoes decorated with woollen fluffing made in Rajouri district.

Following page
Bakarwal family in a tent, Pahalgam, Kashmir

A nomadic family settles for the night. After pitching their tent they make a soft flooring out of fir leaves and squat on it after stacking their saddles, sacks and blankets against the tent wall. Though young men and children have taken to a slightly more contemporary mode of dress, the men still retain their traditional finery. The young boy is setting his transistor to listen to a Gujjar programme which is specially broadcast every day.

features. They have a strong clannish tendency though of late this is wearing thin. Their clan chief functions both as a secular and religious leader and the Gujjars repose unstinted faith in him.

A Gujjar male wears a loose, collarless shirt, *kurta*, a pair of loose pyjamas and a white cloth turban, one edge of which is draped on the left shoulder. A waistcoat tailored from thick cloth is an essential part of his wardrobe and he covers himself with a handwoven *loi* or blanket to ward off the cold.

Women generally wear a *suttan*, a loose gathered pyjama and a decorative *kurta* or shirt that reaches below their knees. The *kurta* is made either of stark black cotton cloth to match the *suttan* or of printed cloth resembling chintz, with tiny sprays of flowers dotting black, navy or dark green fabric. The chest and cuff areas of the shirt are decorated with embroidery done by machine by local tailors according to the instructions of the client. Red and gold ribbons, white ricrac and metallic thread adorn the neck, sleeves and joins of the *kurta* and provide an ornamental setting for the heavy silver jewellery worn by the Bakarwal and Gujjar women. Most of the nomadic women also wear a tailored cap called a *lachka* which is stitched and embroidered by the women. Close-fitting, with a flap extending down to the neck at the back, the *lachka* is a distinctive feature of the nomads. Similar caps are worn by children in communities of the same origin in the desert areas of Gujarat and Rajasthan. Some *lachkas* are embroidered in cotton thread and imitate the fine crissscross *sindhi* stitch of Gujarat and Pakistan or the chain stitch of Kashmir. The skilled needlewoman will choose her threads and colours meticulously while others use thick woollen threads and an awl to boldly decorate their caps with the chain stitch seen on the tapestry fabric of Kashmir. The designs are mostly geometric with circles, triangles, wave-like lines and interlocking figures of eight. Specks of metallic ornamentation may be added to the embroidery while others attach buttons, amulets, coins, shells and beads to decorate the *lachkis* worn by children.

All Bakarwal and Gujjar women wear a *chipra* or head cloth which is usually a printed square of fabric or a light woollen shawl. It is, however, not mandatory for them to wear the *chipra* at all times and it has consequently not evolved as a decorative or important accessory.

Detail of embroidered decoration on Bakarwal blanket

When the rough hand-spun and hand-woven blankets are worn out, they are cut and made into sacks to carry clothing. Simple satin stitch in woollen thread imitates the triangles of the *phulkari* embroidery of Punjab. Bright pinks and oranges are the most popular colours with the nomads.

Far right

Gujjar mother with her child, Pahalgam, Kashmir

The woman wears an embroidered cap, *lachka*, which is made of coarse cloth locally called *soof*, on which she has embroidered a geometric and floral design of chain stitch with silk thread. The cap, half covered with a pink *odhni*, or head cloth, is specific to Allaiwal Bakarwals. It has a short and pointed tail at the back unlike the long flap with a straight edge as in the *lachka* of Kunhari women.

The child's cap has side flaps and is also embroidered in the same floral design with additional embellishments of buttons and silver coins. Sometimes, small conch shells are fixed to ward off the evil eye.

The necklace worn by the woman is called *duldo* and consists of three strings with silver beads. The lower string has hangings of bells and chains. The *duldo* can weigh up to 30 *tolas* and is among the more expensive ornaments worn by Gujjar women. The nose ring is called *dunli* or *laong* and is made of gold or silver with an impregnated stone. Smaller nose rings are called *tilo* or *konka*.

The nomad woman's hairstyle consists of innumerable tiny braids and ornamental hair clips either engraved or decorated with a length of short chains to highlight them. Such specialised jewellery has given rise to a number of silversmiths along the nomad routes who cater to the particular needs of the nomadic people and their traditions. Correspondingly, the Gujjars and Bakarwals have adopted certain objects and made them exclusively their own.

The Gujjar woman wears a large gold nose ornament or *laong* embedded with bright glass or semiprecious stones to display her marital status. The most vital and eye-catching part of her ornamentation however, is the *taveez* and *janzeer*, an elaborate chain and button arrangement to secure the upper portion of the *kurta*. The *taveez* at the neck is the first button of the garment. It is usually square and the stone affixed between the pure silver frame is chosen by the wearer from the silversmith's collection. The *zanjeer* connecting the buttons is about four inches long and hangs from this *taveez*. Longer chains from under the *taveez* extend below to the next two buttons.

Earrings consisting of silver chains corresponding to the *taveez* in length and design are worn on special occasions by some Bakarwal women.

Nomad jewellery made of brass, silver or white metal, has a bold, dramatic quality typical of folk and tribal jewellery worn all over India. Rings are usually large and bright with shining silver paper in red, green or blue placed under glass and framed with a border in metal. Bangles or *kangan* are in engraved metal as well as in filigree with floral motifs and are made by silversmiths at Rajouri and Bhaderwah in the Jammu region along the routes of regular nomadic movement.

Gujjar and Bakarwal women do not wear anklets to adorn their feet and instead wear embroidered leather *mojris* or slip-on shoes decorated with a large red woollen pompom. They are sturdy and hand made by cobblers in Rajouri.

Apart from embroidering their own caps, Bakarwal women also embroider their saddle cloths and the large bags or *chats* that are slung over the backs of ponies. It is here that the creativity of the nomadic person finds expression, and craftsmanship which is both indigenous and individual is manifested.

Banihara Gujjar woman with all her finery, Kakhyal, Kathua

The most prominent adornment is the nose ring, called *laong* or *chargul* in the Jammu region. It is finely worked in gold and bears a large, semiprecious blue stone. The *jhumka* or hanging earring is worn only after marriage. Here again, semiprecious stones or beads are used to ornament the gold or silver. The *duldo* or beaded necklace is typical of the woman's clan. The embroidered shirt and head-cloth are purchased from the local market.

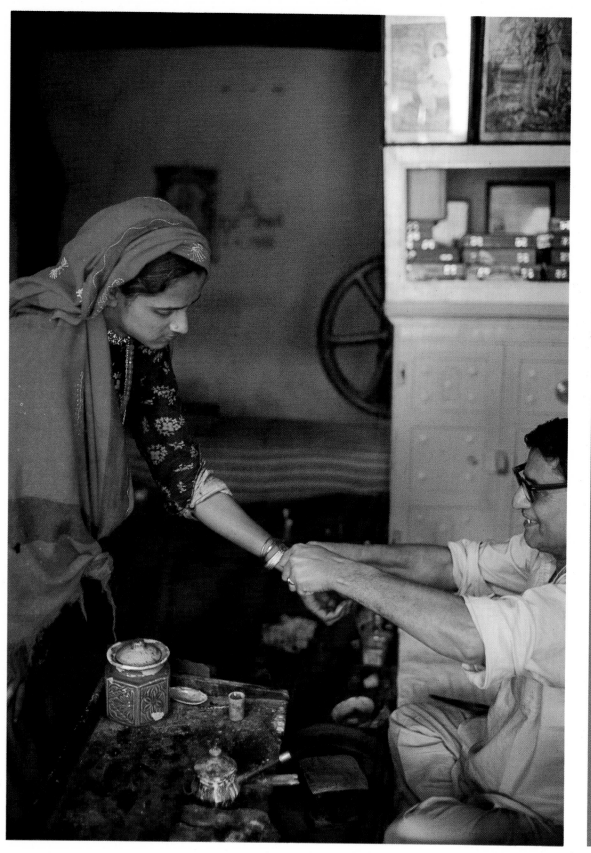
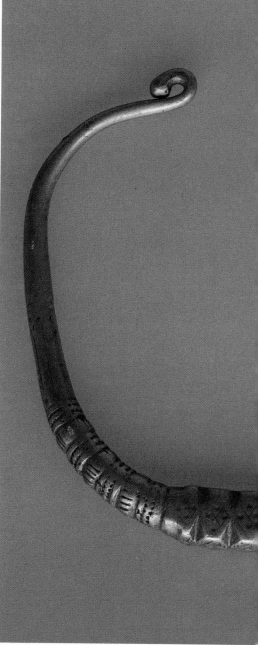

Rough, handspun goat's wool blankets come brilliantly to life with bold, imaginative, asymmetrical designs reflecting in them the various influences felt by the constantly moving Bakarwal clan. Geometric patterns of lines, squares and triangles worked in woollen threads in bold oranges, pinks, greens and yellows cover the surface of these blankets. While no written or oral history explaining the nature of these motifs exists, it is probably not incorrect to surmise that the cross-cultural currents of exchanged folklore with the Gaddis of Himachal Pradesh, the triangles of the bold *phulkari* embroidery of the Punjab, the near geometric flowers of stems of Kashmir embroidery, the attempt at symmetrical layouts and the use of the vivid, rustic colours of the plains, all guide the nomadic woman's hand as she embroiders the rough blankets or coarse cotton remnants of floor coverings to create ornamental sacks.

The blankets themselves are woven by weavers whom the nomads approach along their way. Wool from their goats is given on the journey uphill. When they return, they collect the blanket woven for them in return for a goat, some milk, butter or cheese. Gujjar and Bakarwal men prefer the bright colours of the Punjab village folk, and often dye their goats' wool orange, pink or red before having their blankets woven with it. Men use their meagre and precious leisure moments to fashion rope, netting, pack lashings and reins out of goats' wool. These, too, are often brightly coloured. Tough and long lasting, they demonstrate the basic ingredients of the origin of any craft, viz., the use of local material, human imagination and skill to make an item of utility attractive.

The nomads patronise many of the local crafts during the course of their transhumance. The use of the finely decorated wooden combs of Thana Mandi near Poonch in the Jammu region, and the wooden lathe-turned ladles of Anantnag in the Kashmir valley, the copper dishes of Srinagar and the dress styles of the Punjab demonstrate the unusual and integrating character of the nomadic Gujjars and Bakarwals of this state as they crisscross back and forth, borrowing, returning, giving and taking from crafts and cultures and drawing the invisible thread of all these into themselves as a unique race.

Far left

Gujjar woman in a jeweller's shop, Kathua

A Banihara Gujjar woman buys a bracelet at a jeweller's shop in Kathua town. Jewellers in Riasi, Bardharwah, Kathua and Samba specialise in making ornaments worn only by Gujjars and Bakarwals.

Silver necklace or *hansli* worn by Allaiwal Bakarwals

A necklace or *hansli* made of silver and worn by married women. It is now rarely used because of its prohibitive cost. This ornament originally came from the Allai area of Hazara in Pakistan, from where the Allaiwal group of Bakarwals migrated.

Straw, Willow & Grasswork

The use of straw, grass and twigs to form containers and mats dates back to the earliest days of artisanship when stone gave rise to flints and the earth offered itself for the fashioning of clay bowls. The first attempts at weaving must have been from materials growing wild in lakes and forests. A pot discovered in Mohenjodaro, a site of the Indus Valley civilisation of 3000 B.C., has impressions of a coarse mat on its base and at Burzahom in Kashmir, reed mat weaves have been noted on the excavated pottery.

Settled farmers who needed containers to hold and transport agricultural produce were universal users of baskets and tribal communities with their intimate and deeply spiritual relationship with forests were among the first producers of baskets. Where tribal inhabitants were not known villagers took to making rough baskets for their needs.

In those areas of Jammu and Kashmir rich in vegetation around lakes, swamps and forests, using local grasses, straw and wicker for basketry and matting was the natural result of an agriculture and horticulture based economy.

While basketry has never been acclaimed or considered an important activity, it is perhaps one of the oldest and most basic crafts, and is closely integrated with the daily lives of the people, spanning all classes, communities and religions.

The *kangri* or fire pot is a small, quaint earthenware bowl, held in a frame of decoratively woven willow. Used constantly by the Kashmiris in the winter months and even during rainy summer evenings, the *kangri* is usually slipped under the *pheran* or tunic worn by men and women. The harmonious marriage of willow with clay to create a chafing vessel is mentioned in the *Rajatarangini* (Book V, Verse 106). The verse speaks of the rule of King Avanti Varman between A.D. 855 and 883 when Suyya, the great engineer, skillfully regulated the course of the Vitasta, the Jhelum river. Because of these efforts Kashmir was saved from devastating floods for many years. Suyya kept the waters out by means of circular dykes which gave these villages the appearance of round bowls, *kundas*. Hence the people called these villages Kundala. A footnote to the text says, "The word *kundal* from *sha kundala*, or rings, is still used in Kashmir as the designation of the round earthenware bowl placed in the *Kangar* (*kashtangarika*)". *Kind* in Kashmiri means a large enclosure containing the smouldering fire and *kangri* is the diminutive form of the word.

At a later stage the clay pot baked in a kiln was lined on the outside with twigs of the supple white willow to facilitate holding it while moving about. Three types of forest willow are used to make the *kangri*: the *kui* or *Cotoneaster*, *poshkani* or *Parrotia jacquemontiana* and *kats* or *Indigoferra heternatha*. The local white willow is used in its original form of rounded, unskinned strips.

The local basketmaker in Kashmir is called *shaksaz* or *kainyal* and the most famous locality of wicker weavers is Shaksaz Mohalla in Chirar-e-Sharif. This is a town known for the Nund Rishi shrine, the architectural masterpiece of Kashmiri woodcraft. The most elegant and elaborate *kangris* in the valley are produced here. The wicker is often dyed in blue, green and red shades and various geometric patterns are produced by multi-directional weaves on the upper half of the main body of the *kangri*. Certain portions are left open to insert shiny coloured foil along with mirrors encircled in coloured metal. *Kangris* have from two to seven rows of designs on their upper halves and their price depends

Previous page

Weaving of *waggu* mats, Ganderbal, Kashmir

Willow forests around Ganderbal and large quantities of reed mace in the nearby river make it a centre for mat weaving and basketry. While the willow baskets are used by shoppers and tourists, the *waggu* mat is an intrinsic part of the life of the common man of Kashmir. Wooden pegs are fixed into the earth and rope made of the grass forms the warp, while the flat long blades of grass are woven to form a thick pliable mat, usually two metres long and one and a half metres wide.

Ceremonial *kangri* to be carried by a bride at her wedding

A bridal *kangri* is decorated with many *zals* or rings, circular mirrors and willow chains. The metallic spoon to stir the embers will also be carved. Tassels in coloured willow are a typical form of ornamentation in such work. The *kangri* is an example of how creative embellishment of utility crafts is an intrinsic part of a craftsman's heritage.

on the number of these woven rounds. Bridal *kangris* are named after the number of rounds — *ze-zal*, *tre-zal*, *tror-zal*, on till *sath-zal* or seven chains. Anantnag and Bandipur *kangris* are simpler and of different designs.

The special *kangris* in Chirar-e-Sharif are an important part of ritual occasions observed by the Kashmiri Pandits or Brahmins who celebrate the festival of Shushur Sankrant on the coldest day of January. *Shushur* means frost and on this day the new bride of each family is gifted an ornamental *kangri* which contains some money. Every Hindu family gives the priest a *kangri* to pay homage to its ancestors and family ancestors are supposedly comforted by their descendants in this ritualistic manner. The priests collect a large number of *kangris* which they then sell.

The first Technical Institute in Srinagar was established in 1914-16 and its first principal was a Mr. Andrews, an Englishman. He introduced the English willow in and around the marshes of Bage-Dilawar Khan and the English method of wicker-weaving in the Institute. After steaming and boiling, the willow sheds its thin skin to reveal a pleasing and smooth, pale brick-red surface. Mr. Andrews' students who took to the profession after completing their training used this material to make western-style baskets and boxes. Today, the most extensive English willow fields are the vast areas of Ganderbal and the semi-marsh lands near the northern limits of Anchar lake. As a result, wicker-weaving is concentrated in nearby areas. Another focus of activity is near Hazratbal, the famous shrine at Srinagar where the hair of the Prophet Mohammad is treasured.

Willow or wickerwork is also carried out in Bader-wah, a small, quiet town in Doda district in the Jammu region. The twigs are the same as those used in Kashmir and grow abundantly in the neighbouring forests. The *kathi* or willow bush stands one to 1.5 metres high and is collected from the forests between June and October. Apples, walnuts, apricots and the red pea lentil of this region are sent to different areas of the state in traditional willow baskets and trays which are woven in a particular street of Doda town called Qilla Mohalla. The large basket is locally called *kiltu*.

The outer layer of *kathi* sticks is removed with the help of two round wooden sticks. They are then left out in the dew for at least four to five nights. This

***Kangri* making at Shaksaz Mohalla, Chirar-e-Sharif, Kashmir**

All members of a family engage in the production of *kangris*. While men gather, strip and soak the willow, the women dye the strips in bright colours. Men and women helped by their children weave a variety of designs for both everyday and ceremonial use.

Far right

***Kangri* seller at Shaksaz Mohalla, Chirar-e-Sharif, Kashmir**

The *kangri* of Chirar-e-Sharif is the most admired of all the chafing pots used to ward off the cold in Kashmir. Made of clay and enveloped in intricate willow weaves, it is used for weddings and other festive occasions. The *kangri* is held close to the body under the *pheran* or shawl and enables people to move about freely. Smouldering coal covered with the ash of semi-burnt *chinar* leaves inside the clay bowl provides ample warmth, while the willow covering allows it to be held without discomfort.

Willow *karkhana* and retail shop, Srinagar

A wide variety of willow basketry is carried out in Srinagar and its environs, extending up to Ganderbal which has extensive willow plantations. The locality surrounding the famed Hazratbal mosque in Srinagar is dotted with shops where craftsmen produce baskets, picnic hampers and lamp shades. They are also able to copy the most elaborate designs in willow furniture from simple photographs and drawings.

Far right

Raw material for willow work

The willow is steamed and boiled until its skin is shed, leaving the exposed layer smooth and brick-red in colour. Simple tools to skin and cut it further, a bowl of water to soak the willow for softness during weaving, and skilled fingers are all that is needed to make these long strips of willow into handsome baskets.

Reed mace collected from the edges of Nagin Lake to make *waggu* matting

The *waggu* matting used as roofing on boats and flooring in homes is woven by villagers in the open spaces surrounding their homes. Even children, who learn to row at an early age, collect *pits* or reed mace, the grass used for these mats. The Nagin lake in Srinagar has an abundance of *pits* in its waters.

Women prepare rope to weave *waggu* matting, Ganderbal, Kashmir

The narrow strips of grass are wound around the toe and twisted before tying them across to form the warp of a *waggu* mat.

Far right
***Pulahru* or straw shoe from Kishtwar, Sri Pratap Singh Museum, Srinagar**

Wheat straw woven into fine rope is fashioned into shoes and decorated with coloured threads on the upper half. These were used in the remote hilly region of Kishtwar where most journeys were undertaken on foot over wet and slippery terrain. Earlier, for outdoor use, inhabitants of the entire Himalayan region wore different versions of this design in straw shoes. Felt and woollen shoes with straw soles were worn indoors by both men and women.

Following page
Detail of wheat straw basket, Kishtwar

The lustrous light golden shade of the wheat grown in Kishtwar lends a natural sheen to a basket woven for home use.

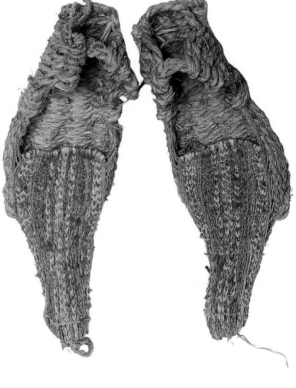

renders them white and shiny and flexible enough to be easily woven. Prior to being woven the sticks are soaked in water for two hours and they are coloured either before or after weaving.

Matting is said to have been introduced in Kashmir by Mirza Haider Daughlat in the 16th century. The reed mace, a swamp plant locally called *pits* (*Typha sp.*), is used to make excellent matting called *waggu*. *Pits* is found in most swamps and grows in abundance around the Dal and Nagin lakes of Srinagar.

The Anchar lagoon to the north of Srinagar is the great home of this rush grass. The villagers of Lasjan, south of Srinagar, are perhaps the best mat makers. All small boats are roofed with the tough yet supple *waggu* and it is also used as a floor matting in boats and houses. *Waggu* is often used as an under-carpet to provide extra warmth in winter. Laid out from wall to wall, it is covered with a printed cotton *masnad* or floor covering, or thicker woollen *gabbas* or *numdahs*.

The ordinary footwear of the Kashmiri has always been made of leather, wood or straw. The straw sandal is called *tsapli* or *pulahru* and every Kashmiri made his own *pulahru* out of rice straw while the people from Kishtwar wore ornamental straw shoes with coloured threads and pompoms. There were many differences in dress between the Muslims and Hindus, one being that Hindu women, unlike their Muslim counterparts, always wore grass sandals, never leather ones.

There is an amusing Kashmiri saying which refers to the lowly grass shoe: "*Rasmut pula har sheht mohur*" which means "He has also lost his grass shoes and claims seven gold *mohurs* as compensation"! This indicates that the Kashmiri is known to exaggerate his losses although he underestimates his possessions. Grass shoes have been commonly worn for hundreds of years by the poor coolies or pack porters of Kashmir, Kishtwar and Bhaderwah while a sophisticated and ornamental version was worn by the upper classes.

The straw sandals enabled pack carriers, farmers who lived near the foothills, and those who negotiated muddy, rocky and glacial terrain to maintain a firm grip on slippery surfaces without adding much weight to their feet.

Bamboo forests in the Shivalik range of hills provide material for basket weaving to the craftsmen

Gathering dung in a willow basket, Ladakh

The vast treeless expanse resembling the surface of the moon makes every piece of dung or stray twig important as a source of fuel. *Malchang*, the local term for the willow, is obtained from the trees planted alongside streams flowing through villages. Willow baskets are extensively used as pack containers in every rural household in Ladakh.

community in Kathua district in the Jammu region. These simple and functional baskets are an integral part of the everyday life of the rural people and of the local bazaar where they are piled roof-high and attract attention with their bright yellow and pink daubs of paint.

The fertile soil of Kishtwar, also in the Jammu region, produces an equally exceptional quality of wheat known for its lustrous and light golden straw. In Kishtwar, prayer mats and baskets made of this straw are delicately decorated with bright woollen strands of thread.

Ladakh, with its majestic but sparsely vegetated topography, depends almost exclusively on baskets of grass and willow, locally called *malchang*, to transport goods. Areas such as Kargil, Bod Kharbu, Lamayuru, Saspol and Nimmo are well-planted with willow trees near the rivers and streams. Conical and square-bottomed baskets are used by every household. These baskets are tied to the back with ropes woven from goat's hair and are used to carry anything from a small child and twigs for fuel to the dung of the local *zo* or *zomo*, mud and clay pots.

A local reed called *chipkiang* grows near villages such as Chushot, close to the Indus river. A pale gold soft grass, *chipkiang* is widely used to make pack baskets. Women use them to carry turnips, radishes, spinach and cauliflower from their small, cultivated patches to the bazaar of Ladakh's capital, Leh.

The *chipkiang* grass is first soaked in water for some hours before being woven by men in their homes. The smaller basket called *tsepo* is generally used to carry vegetables and fertilisers while the bigger basket, *phukstel*, is used for carrying grass and fodder. When the *chipkiang* is woven into matting for use in homes it is called *shakstar*.

Till today the people of Ladakh have found no better way of carrying goods than in these baskets, securely bound to their backs, leaving their hands free to operate a spindle, knit socks or to rotate the prayer wheel while carrying their burden.

Far left
Vegetable market, Leh, Ladakh

Baskets, *tsepo*, made of grass grown near the Indus river, are woven by the men while women transport home-grown vegetables in them for sale in the heart of town. Women don a high-domed hat, *tibi*, embroidered with metallic thread for daily wear and their hands are constantly occupied with spinning local wool.

A mother carries her child in a willow basket, Ladakh

The use of local materials for most needs is necessitated in Ladakh by its geographical isolation. The local willow is both strong and pliant and a willow basket makes a safe carrier for small children.

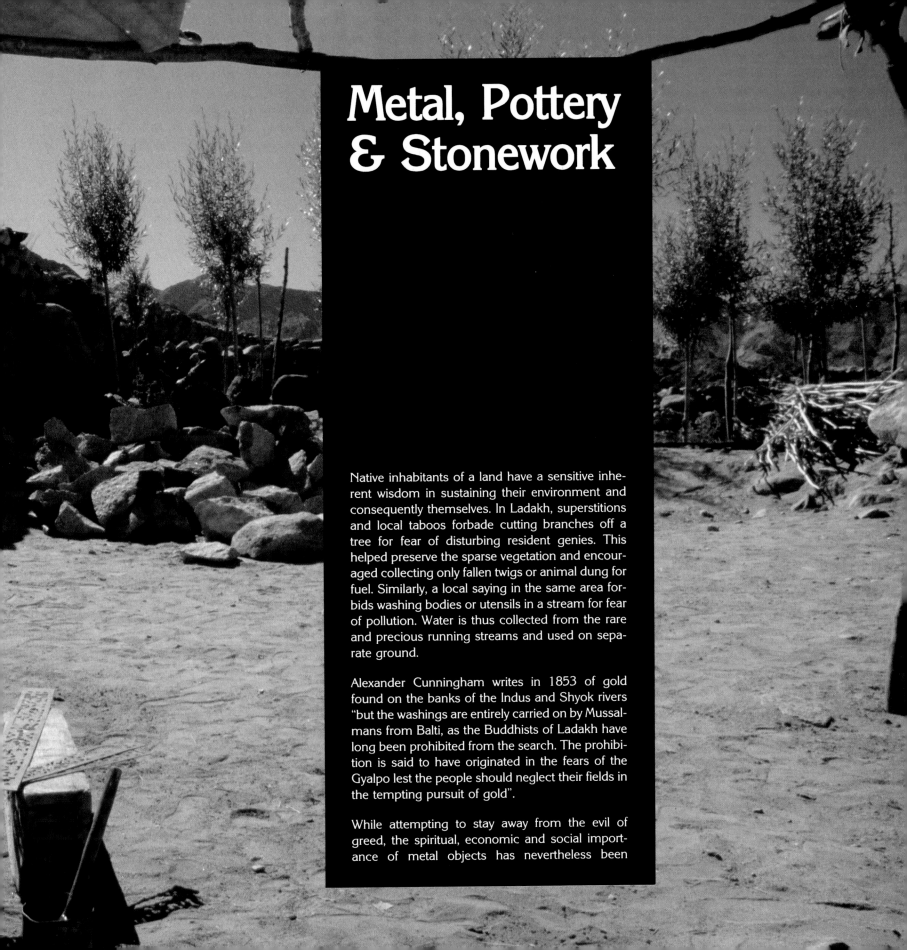

Metal, Pottery & Stonework

Native inhabitants of a land have a sensitive inherent wisdom in sustaining their environment and consequently themselves. In Ladakh, superstitions and local taboos forbade cutting branches off a tree for fear of disturbing resident genies. This helped preserve the sparse vegetation and encouraged collecting only fallen twigs or animal dung for fuel. Similarly, a local saying in the same area forbids washing bodies or utensils in a stream for fear of pollution. Water is thus collected from the rare and precious running streams and used on separate ground.

Alexander Cunningham writes in 1853 of gold found on the banks of the Indus and Shyok rivers "but the washings are entirely carried on by Mussalmans from Balti, as the Buddhists of Ladakh have long been prohibited from the search. The prohibition is said to have originated in the fears of the Gyalpo lest the people should neglect their fields in the tempting pursuit of gold".

While attempting to stay away from the evil of greed, the spiritual, economic and social importance of metal objects has nevertheless been

Previous page
A blacksmith works outdoors, Sabu, Ladakh

The blacksmiths are an exclusive community known as *gara* who manufacture iron stoves, locks and keys and also fashion conch bangles. Their highly ornamental stoves are in great demand with the local population.

Far left
***Thap chabrik*, iron stove unit, Leh, Ladakh**

The *piece de resistance* of the *gara* or blacksmith community, the stove is decorated with brass ornaments and contains an oven and a tray to remove ash. The kitchen is the pride of every family in Ladakh. Brass and copper ladles, silver tea bowl covers, water jugs and cooking vessels are all made by the *sergar* or silversmith. On the extreme left is the *gud gud*, the onamatopoeic name for the long cylindrical wood and brass tea-maker in which tea, milk and butter are churned, producing a deep rhythmic sound.

Detail of blacksmith making strips of brass with motifs to decorate an iron stove, Sabu, Ladakh

Brass strips are cut in a variety of traditional designs considered of religious or auspicious significance. These are attached to stoves, doorways, boxes and any other item considered worthy of decoration.

reflected throughout Ladakh in the decorative figures and ornaments, liturgical objects and household articles made by its craftspeople.

The earliest mention of a metal object according to Cunningham, was the Tibetan prayer wheel, by "Chinese pilgrim Fa Hien in A.D. 400, who saw it in the hands of Sramanas of Kie-Chha (Ladak)".

These prayer wheels and other religious objects made of copper and brass embellished with silver are made by the *sergars* or silversmiths of Ladakh. They also make the sparkling tea pots, *chhang* pots, bowls, ladles and other utensils that decorate the shelves of each kitchen and, after jewellery, are the pride of every Ladakhi household.

The best known *sergars* live in Chiling, a two-day journey on horseback from Leh. In winter, walking over the frozen Zangskar river makes the trip easier. The artisans of Chiling are among those rare people who are able to trace their arrival at this spot to a specific point in time. According to them, kings Deldan Namgyal and Sengge Namgyal sent the first artisans there in the latter half of the 17th century. They, in turn, identified the most suitable spot by unleashing an arrow which fell at a particular location. There they found both wood and native copper, (*zang* in Zangskar in fact means copper), and were thus able to set up abode to pursue their professional work. Today, their descendants are wealthy and their artefacts are prized by the aristocracy of Ladakh.

The blacksmith in Ladakh is part of an exclusive community called *gara* which is comparable to the *kami*, the blacksmith of the Hindu community, and similar groups considered as a lower caste in Tibet. Like the Gadiya Lohars of Rajasthan, Ladakhi blacksmiths often go from house to house with their tools, repairing old metal objects, galvanising them or installing the large iron stoves — *thap chabrik* — complete with ovens, grills, ashtrays, brass ornamentation and perhaps even the price tag carefully cut out and attached as part of the decoration. The *gara* also make agricultural implements and are well known for the manufacture of locks unique in design. These locks contain nine to sixteen lever mechanisms and their shapely ornamental keys are worn suspended from the waist by a silver chain or a length of string.

Traditional customary practice assigns a special role to the *gara* in Ladakhi society. At the birth of a child, the *gara* give a newborn girl two metal bracelets, while a boy is given a small metal bow and arrow which is pinned to his back. As a part of custom they visit at the New Year, offering a needle in exchange for a meal and when someone dies they repair the family jewellery.

Decorative designs commonly used by the *gara* are: two dragons facing each other, *druk khabrel*; a floral strip, *tanka*, similar to those found on old Chinese coins, the Ladakhi cap and on brocade cloth; *gyanak chagri*, also found on *Mani* walls, carpet borders and on the edges of socks; *yumdum-lagyut*, used mostly in prayer room decorations; and the geometric lucky diagram, *palpyu*, a relic of the pre-Buddhist Bönpa religion. The *dorjay* or thunderbolt, a sceptre, is the most popular design and copies a ritualistic instrument. Cunningham explains it as "the *Vajra* of the Indians — a holy instrument said to have flown away from India and to have alighted in Sera, in Tibet. That it was looked upon in India as an object of reverence, or as an emblem of power is proved by its being placed in the right hand of a raja in the Sanchi bas-reliefs."

The *sergar* and the *gara* use hand-operated bellows for their work. The *gara* has now replaced leather bellows for metal and works with a handle and propellers which blow the air along two pipes hollowed out in the ground up to the fire grate. Simple tools such as tongs, a hammer, pliers and scissors are used to heat and hammer, cut or bend objects into shape. Superficial decoration is done by cutting designs out of a brass sheet with a hammer and large nail. The *sergar* still uses bellows made of animal skin, occasionally fanning the grate while the object is manipulated and shaped above the burning coal. Often, the client will help the *gara* and *sergar* in operating the bellows.

Except for a deep, russet-hued quality of copper that comes from Zangskar, all other metals came into Ladakh from Tibet and are now supplied from other regions in India. The *gara* has to spend most of his time repairing objects and otherwise obtains his raw material by dismantling old metal containers and drums while the rising costs of precious metals have made the *sergars'* items prized possessions of their owners.

Lady holding chhos-khor or prayer wheel made by a sergar, Ladakh

Alexander Cunningham describes the prayer wheel as "a metal cylinder about three inches in height ... The axis is prolonged below to form a handle ... and the cylinder is filled with rolls of printed prayers and charms, which revolve as the instrument is turned round. Every Lama carries a *chhos-khor* which he keeps perpetually turning by a gentle motion of the hand, assisted by a cubical piece of iron fastened by a chain to the outside. As every revolution of a prayer is equivalent to its recitation, the *chhos-khor* is a very ingenious instrument for multiplying the number of a man's prayers."

Brass and wood *hukka* base and *chillum*, early 20th century, Ladakh

The finely wrought brass decoration on a lathe-turned and hand-carved wooden base indicates the high quality of workmanship of early 20th century silversmiths from Chiling.

Far right

Copper, brass, silver and gold-plated tea kettle; late 19th century; from the private collection of 'Kahlon' Rigzin Namgyal; Zangskar, Ladakh

Made by a *sergar* of Chiling the central medallion affixed to the body of the kettle is *Chya Tsering*, an auspicious figure. The handle is given the form of a dragon and the spout assumes a mythical elephant's head. Fine filigree decorates the base. The deep colour of the copper indicates that it is from Zangskar.

Kartak, ceremonial tea bowl, from the private collection of 'Kahlon' Rigzin Namgyal, Ladakh

This tea bowl has a gold and silver stand and a lid with coral beads. The designs have been finely carved by a silversmith of Chiling. The *gyanakchagri* motif forms the border at the base and the ceremonial *padma*, lotus, can be seen on the central layer of the lid.

Sergar or silversmith of Chiling at work in Leh, Ladakh

Pumping sheepskin bellows, the silversmith makes brass and copper ladles, *chhang* pots, kettles and bowls

Inset

Detail of *sergar*, silversmith, decorating the silver lid of a tea bowl, Ladakh

Tea drinking is a constant and almost ceremonial occupation in the cold winter months. For honoured guests on festive occasions fine china tea bowls are covered with ornamental lids to keep the tea warm.

Following page

A kitchen at Likir, Ladakh

Likir is well known for its famous monastery which controls the monastery at Alchi. It is also the home of many potters and woodworkers. This kitchen belongs to a wood carver who happens to make clay stoves as well. The large iron stove lends warmth to the kitchen which becomes the congregating point for the entire family on long winter evenings. Brass vessels adorn the shelves and the kitchen attains the status of a living room.

Jammu's most typical and traditional metalcraft is the casting of large vessels, particularly those used for cooking during weddings and other festive occasions. When factory-made steel and aluminium utensils were still unknown, the entire village of Badiyal Brahmana in Ranbirsinghpura was engaged in this work and the harsh but rhythmic clash and clatter of metal casting and the repairing and beating of brass and copper deafened those who traversed the narrow lanes of Moti Bazaar in Jammu city.

In villages the *gagar* is used for storing water, the *baltoi* for cooking *dal* and the *sagla* for rice. The technique employed is the *cire pérdue* method in which wax is layered between two moulded coatings of mud. It is then heated so that it pours out through an opening below. Molten brass is poured from the top into the empty space vacated by the wax. When it cools and solidifies, the outer covering of mud is broken away, revealing the brass vessel.

Vessels weigh between 16 to 25 kgs each and the progress of time can be assessed by a comparison in costs. Fifty years ago, a *sagla* cost between Rs.18 to Rs.20 a piece, while today, sold by weight, a *sagla* can cost up to Rs.800, at Rs.32 per kg.

The use of metals in Kashmir dates back to the neolithic period. A number of metal objects, including beads and arrow-heads, were found at Burzahom. Kalhana speaks highly of the metalware of Kashmir which appears to have been one of the few areas in the country where brass was a more favoured item than bronze. Most ancient bronzes were hollow and at times surface details were chased and polished after the objects were cast.

Kashmiri craftsmen were equally great masters in inlay work, as is revealed by various bronzes preserved in different museums the world over. Inlay was often done on the garments of bronze figures in order to create a rich surface texture, and it is likely that the technique was transported to Eastern Persia through Ghazni around the 11th century. Interestingly, inlaid brass became the favoured medium of Persian metallurgy after the 11th century. Kalhana records details of the commissioning of colossal gold, silver and bronze images of various deities during Lalitaditya's reign which witnessed an artistic renaissance in metal work in Kashmir. After his coronation, King Avantivarman (ninth

century) is reported to have renounced all his material wealth and melted the gold and silver vessels in his treasury. Kalhana reports that various metal images were melted down by subsequent rulers during economic crises and also makes frequent references to kings and other royal personalities eating food off gold and silver plates. These literary references provide sufficient proof of the religious and domestic use of various metals in ancient Kashmir.

Copper was locally mined during medieval times and is reported to have been extracted from the mountains of Aishmuqam and at Lsytiyal in the Lolab valley. King Zain-ul-Abadin is said to have met his entire private expenditure from the proceeds of a copper mine which he discovered in Kashmir. In his famous *Tarikh Rashidi*, Mirza Haider Daughlat wrote, "In Kashmir one meets with all those arts and crafts which are in most cities uncommon, such as stone polishing, stone cutting, bottle making, gold beating, etc. In the whole of Marv-ul-Nahr, the country beyond the river Oxus i.e. Khorasam except Samarqand and Bokhara these are nowhere to be met with. While in Kashmir they are even abundant." The richness of the craft is attributed to Zain-ul-Abadin. Moorecroft, while visiting the valley in 1823 made frantic efforts to learn where the copper mines of Kashmir were situated but was informed by the artisans that it was a carefully guarded secret lest the Sikh rulers discovered it and exploited the copper as a source of revenue.

Most of the early medieval metalwork bears simple engraved decoration, the majority of metal being left plain. Vessels engraved with designs consisted mainly of arabesque figures of animals and calligraphic inscriptions. Later, a more elaborate form of decoration employing inlay was developed.

During the Mughal era, metalwork concentrated on the making of swords and gun-barrels, which were then damascened and enamelled. By the end of the 19th century, gunmaking declined and the forging of swords and blades had altogether ceased. Consequently, the hereditary skill of the Kashmir metal workers was directed towards ornamental vessels such as the *aftaba*, *surahi* and other such items of domestic use.

While the shape of these ancient vessels belongs to the Indo-Persian tradition as a whole, the decora-

Copper milk vessel with engraving, contemporary, Kashmir

Milk is transported to cities from villages in large copper vessels which are loaded onto donkeys, horses, carriages, cycles or buses. Made in Zainakadal, Srinagar, these vessels are decorated with Persian calligraphy, interspersed with bands of *chinar* leaf patterns, ferns and cypress leaves and have become a popular artefact for export.

Copper engraving at Zainakadal, Srinagar

Copper is still the most popular metal for household use in Kashmir. A *samovar*, *surahi*, *aftaba* or *hukka* may be proudly displayed in the corner of a living room and used for honoured guests. Craftsmen use simple tools and often work in ill-lit rooms producing exquisite works of art.

Far right

Copper ladle with carved handle at the Juma bazaar, Hazratbal, Srinagar

Plain, beaten, embossed or engraved, copper is used to make a variety of utensils for both daily and festive occasions.

tion is usually of Kashmiri inspiration. Perhaps the most attractive and certainly the best items are produced in copper and the most popular ones include the *lota, samawar* and *farsh tram*. The *sun tram paila* is made in six styles, the *toor* in four and the *kenz* in three sizes. Ornamental tumblers, *teliwar, isbandsoz, majma, chamcha*, and lately *paila nor* and *bati chalan* have been added to the traditional items. These are all items of daily utility in the kitchen and include ladles in various sizes, dishes, bowls and water containers.

The most important appliances for the manufacture of copper items include *draj, mekh, yandrewah, basta, thaj, sharanz, sheekh, gosheper* and *angus*.

The silver work of Kashmir is extremely beautiful and some of the indigenous patterns, like the *chinar* and lotus leaf, are of exquisite design. Raw silver is mostly imported from other parts of the country and during the medieval period raw material was also provided by the famed caravans of Central Asia that passed through Kashmir.

The production of a silver object involves three stages — preparing it, engraving and, when necessary, cleaning and gilding it.

In all, about five categories of workers are involved in the process. They are the *khar*, smith; *naqash*, engraver; *zarcob*, gilder; *roshangar*, polisher; and *charakgar*, cleaner.

Silversmiths prepare an alloy of pure silver and copper — four per cent is roughly the quantity of copper added — from which the object is hammered and given the required shape. Handles and other complicated parts are fabricated separately before they are joined to the main object. The item is then cleaned with sulphuric acid before it is passed on to the *naqash*, who fills it with lac to make the surface harder. This facilitates executing minute details. The silversmith works with a hammer and chisel and engraves with a pencil. The lac is removed after engraving and the object is cleaned again. At this stage, engravings on one or both sides are done. The object is then cleaned a third and last time which involves an elaborate process of subjecting it repeatedly to fire and water, each time removing the impurities with a brush. Finally, the object is rubbed with "ruby" powder and then polished. If it is to be gilted, it is passed on to the

Silver tray with cutwork and inlay; 18th century; Museum of Central Asian Studies; Kashmir University, Srinagar

Shades of blue and turquoise inlay delicately highlight the fine paisley and flower motifs on this tray. The blue pigment was imported from China and Persia and is said to be the same as that used in the Ajanta frescoes. The turquoise was obtained from local minerals. The tray was presented to the Museum by the state *toshakhana* which stores valuable artefacts previously owned by the erstwhile rulers of the state.

zarcob and then to the *roshangar* for polishing. This job is done entirely by hand to protect the engraving on the surface.

In Kashmir, there are still *mohallas* or localities like the Roshangar Mohalla, and the profession is carried down from generation to generation.

Silversmiths use simple appliances which are locally made by ironsmiths according to their specifications. Some important appliances and forged tools include *iran*, *hathodi*, *angus*, *hundach*, *garwan*, *yandrewah* and *sharanz*, while the *naqash's* tools consist, among others, of the *teeniha* or *kalam* and *ankoonan*. Earlier, the *charakgar* worked with an antiquated hand wheel but he uses a machine today, and the *zarcob's* appliances include the *katore*, *yandrewah* and *poshmech*.

The technique of decorating an object with enamel and a ground glass paste has a long history. The enamelling process consists of applying powdered glass to a metal base of either copper, silver or gold and fusing the two by heating the glass, coloured with finely ground metal oxides. Water is added to make a paste that is usually applied to the metal base with a brush. The ground is chased or engraved with the silver or gold base.

In Kashmir, enamelling is done on silver, copper and brass by fusing various mineral substances. The metal is punched or repoussé for enamelling. This is done by embedding various colours in the depressions or by painting the surface of metallic objects with fusible paint and then subjecting it to an appropriate heat which brings out the colour in a finished form. These colours include salicates, borates, yellow through chromate of potash, violet through carbonate of manganese, blue through cobalt oxide, green through copper oxide and brown through red iron oxide. For enamelling copper, objects different shades of blue are most frequently used while a light blue is applied on silver. The enamelling done on copper and brass is more coarse and not translucent and although it does not crack easily it loses its lustre with the aging of the metal. The patterns are punched, repoussé and the hollows thus produced are filled with a readily fusible glass paint. Traditional shawl patterns have been adopted and appear mostly on vessels, *surahis*, trays and other items where enamelling is combined with gilding. Arabesque, Mosaic and embossed styles are also used.

Detail of metal tumbler; 19th century; School of Design Museum, Kashmir

Made in silver alloy with deep blue enamelling, this tumbler has stylised woodpeckers and other birds placed amongst delicate foliage.

From early times people have been fashioning vessels from baked clay for cooking, eating and storage. The Dards, grave site at Leh, Ladakh, has yielded statues of the neolithic period of the Kashmir valley. Clay statues at Alchi eloquently testify to the potter's talent in shaping various icons out of clay. In Wanla, near Leh, master craftsmen still produce large clay icons painted in bright colours for monasteries.

The Ladakhi potter is among the most simple and primitive of artisans and earns his living by making the various mud bowls, jugs, tea kettles and braziers required in the peasant home. While in the plains of Jammu and in the valley of Kashmir the potter's wheel is used, in Ladakh the potter still moulds his objects by hand, with the help of simple equipment made of wood, stone and leather. Oil lamps and incense burners are often decorated with tiny eyelets arranged like a three-leaf clover. The local barley beer, *chhang*, is stored in the *zama*, a wide vessel, narrowing at the neck and opening again into a wide mouth. The most admirable clay item in the village potter's repertoire is a large tea kettle complete with spout, lid and handle, along with a brazier to keep the contents of the kettle warm.

Kashmir is rich in a variety of clay eminently suitable to the potter's craft which has been practised in the valley since neolithic times. The skillfully made utilitarian wares and their successive levels of development can be traced at the Burzahom and Gofkal sites in Kashmir. The most significant achievement of the neolithic period was the rough grey earthenware with straw marks on its exterior, found in the earliest levels of the structural complex, categorised as dwelling pits. This is perhaps the period in Kashmir when pottery emerged as a source of supplementing the economy of the neolithic people. By 1700 B.C. the potter made systematic and steady progress towards manufacturing different varieties of earthenware including storage jars, lids, feeding-bowls, water pots and small vases — all entirely hand-made. The technique was to put kneaded *karewa* clay in layers around a mass which the potter intended to make, smoothening the surface with a piece of wood or bone and giving a final shape with a dabber. This method continued for nearly a thousand years and it was only during the megalithic period that a variety of pots and other objects were made mainly

through the introduction of the potter's wheel. This happened around 1000 B.C.

The wheel introduced greater plasticity in fabricating narrow and medium-size pots, while maintaining traditional shapes made with more durable ingredients like stone and sand. The present day *math*, *deg*, *tsod* and other vessels are almost replicas of pottery objects used around four thousand years ago.

Many new inventions in the early historical period led to the emergence of different medium-sized pottery. These include the dish-on-stand which is bracketed with objects from the post-Harappan period found at Bara in the Punjab. An important technological improvisation was the introduction of glazed earthenware, commonly known as N.B.P. at the excavation site at Semthan in Bijbehara. N.B.P., or Northern Burnished Pottery, was in vogue in Afghanistan and the North West Province from the fifth to the second centuries B.C. Semthan potters also modelled some beautiful terracotta figures as well as bowls in shapes associated with the deluxe ware of the Nandas of Magadh and the Maurya prototype sites at Kanishpur. This is followed by redware pottery represented by hollow cups, lids and medium-sized pots which continued from the first century A.D. till about the sixth century A.D., falling in the Kushan and post-Kushan period.

The great classical pottery period of Harwan and Ushkar is represented by extraordinary moulded tiles and terracotta heads unique in the entire repertoire of Indian art. Large storage jars with out-turned rims apparently with lids have come from Martand before the construction of the famous Martand temple by Lalitaditya. Enormous storage jars called *math* and medium-sized pottery represented by cooking pots, *handi*, have also been found and are often associated with the temple sites especially of Karkota. Terracotta miniature vases, incense burners, rattles and ladles are among the items bequeathed to us by the master potters of ancient Kashmir.

The Timurid contribution was the development of the glazed tile, an ancient art revived in the Seljuq period. It was in the 15th century that mosaic tiles were made by the Kashmir potter. Panels of coloured glazed tiles were employed both for the interior and exterior of the Madin Sahib mausoleum at Zadibal in Sringar. Colour was thus introduced

Sagla **maker, Jain Bazaar, Jammu**

Large brass vessels made by pouring molten brass into mud moulds is a dying craft of Jammu, practised by a handful of artisans. Here the worker rubs and polishes the *sagla* after the outer mould has been broken away.

Far right

Brass and copper *hamam* or hot water dispenser; mid-20th century, Jammu

Hamams are used on ceremonial occasions to enable guests to wash their hands with hot water after a feast.

into what was otherwise a monotonous surface of plain bricks. Tiles in light green were used on mud floorings. These glazed colour tiles were intended to give added emphasis to the architectonic elements.

The main variation in pottery appeared with the advent of the Mughals who introduced glazed pottery and pots with red slip sprinkled over them, as is revealed from some eating bowls discovered in Haripur, the old Mughal road linking Kashmir to other parts of India.

The traditional *kral* or potter of the valley begins his work by centring a lump of clay on a circular mud wheel head, balancing it firmly on a wooden pivot, in an open space. Working with both hands, he gradually raises the sides of the clay till he achieves the final shape of the pot. It is then detached by a string and dried in the shade before it is baked in the *konda*, a kiln with even heat, where it turns hard, durable and fit for use. Besides manufacturing utilitarian ware, the *kral* also produces certain objects linked with the Shivratri festival. These include the *soni poutul*, *dhoopazoor parwa* and *saniwar*, all of which have a symbolic significance and have retained their shape over time. The potter of Kashmir produced clay containers for the *kangri* or chafing pot widely used as a body warmer, as well as bowls called *kenz*. The *chillum* containing smouldering embers for the ubiquitous *hukka* keeps the potter of Kashmir constantly at work.

In Srinagar today the most durable and popular glazed pottery is manufactured at Rainawari. Commonly known as Dalgate pottery, since the shops which sell tourist items are concentrated there, these vessels are coated with a deep brown or green glaze produced with glass powder. A wide range of glazed pottery items include dinner sets, tea sets, flower vases, *hukkas* and *martabans*. Rural pottery found in Chirar-e-Sharif is painted red and blue and is occasionally decorated with white and green flowers.

Early Harappan pottery found at Manda in Akhnoor in Jammu has added a new dimension to the pottery of the valley since the Harappan urban civilization happened to be contemporaneous with it. The sequence of the pottery at Manda is similar to that found at Rupar, Bara and Banavali. These are represented by the dish-on-stand, beakers, bowls, jars and other prototypes of Harappan pottery. Early

Pottery shop, Chirar-e-Sharif, Kashmir

Earthenware is still very much in demand for home use, particularly in rural areas. Low-priced and colourful clay objects are used to store water, set curd and cook vegetables and meat. A tiny rice bowl, *kenz*, with a stand and high edges is designed so that children can feed themselves conveniently without spilling the grains of rice.

historical pottery is represented by thin to thick red-ware from sites at Mah and Pambarwan in Akhnoor and Rajouri in Jammu. The manufacture of this type of pottery at Jammu is highlighted by the discovery of beautiful terracotta heads found at the Buddhist monastery at Akhnoor. There was a definite change in pottery making with the arrival of the Mughals, clues of which were found on the banks of the river Chenab.

The potter has always been an integral part of the rural economy and still plays an active role in the large areas of the state which are not urbanised. While mud pots for storing water continue to be widely used in every village home, even aristocratic urban homes in Jammu use large earthern storage jars called *math*. Lightly decorated and fired at high temperatures in simple backyard kilns, these vessels last almost a lifetime and are used for storing wheat, rice, sugar and pulses. They stand one metre tall and around 0.75 metre wide. *Koll*, earthern grain containers with folk motifs, and decorated pots and *surahis* prominently display the Jammu potter's ingenuity in handling clay.

Like pottery, stoneware provides indestructible historical evidence of human settlements in the region and forms a landmark in the history of the arts and crafts of Jammu, Kashmir and Ladakh.

Stone has been frequently used in Ladakh to carve huge figures on rock faces or as votive offerings at cross-roads and other conspicuous places. One cannot miss the fine stone carvings of Maitreya, the future Buddha, 12 metres high on a monolithic rock at Mulbeck or the Dyani Buddhas at Shey. The portrayal of Buddhist manifestations in stone is not an isolated phenomenon and indicates an early stone tradition and the maturity of the master carvers. The long Mani walls all over Ladakh, capped with thousands of inscribed stones in variegated colours and shapes, have engaged stone carvers for centuries. Carving turquoise for the ceremonial Ladakhi headdress, cups and other items from precious stones and shaping stones for various ornaments keeps the traditional stone carver busy working at a height of over 3,500 metres above sea level.

The neolithic people of Kashmir fashioned various stone tools which are unique in the context of the stone craft of India. Master stone carvers made delicate stone chisels for carpentry work, complex

Far left

Terracotta grain pots in the store room of a Jammu household

In rural areas, mud pots are used both for cooking and storage. Standing almost 80 cms high the storage *maths* contain wheat, rice and corn and are decorated by womenfolk particularly if they are given or received on auspicious occasions.

Potter, Likir, Ladakh

The traditional potter does not use a wheel and moulds objects by hand. The natural simplicity of his surroundings is reflected in the manner of his work.

tools including the adze, axe, ring stone, grinder, as well as other tools to shape pristine cornelian heads of various shapes for jewellery. An outstanding stone panel from 1700 B.C. with engravings by dextrous stone carvers reveals the full drama of a neolithic hunt. The carver faithfully depicts the interdependence of the elements of nature, animals and human beings represented by two suns, a *Hangul* and dog and a male and female.

In the 1st century A.D. miniature engraved stone seals from Semthan near Bijbehara convey the high level of skill inherent in the stone seal cutter and engraver of that era which continues till today. The work of the 5th century A.D. is best represented by the unusual tantric figure of a Shiva hitherto unknown in the Indian context from Fategarh in Baramula.

Bijbehara sculptures of the sixth century A.D. have a unique place in the history of stone art in Kashmir. The most glorious period of stone art, however, was the Karkota period under Lalitaditya, a great patron of art, who is credited with having built massive stone temples including the Sun Temple at is credited with having built massive stone temples including the Sun Temple at Martand and the temple complex at Parihasapur. The engravings around the Martand temple represent well-modelled figures including various Chinese and Greek elements but within the overall tradition of Indian stone art. Though separated in space and time, the elegant fluted pillars, huge trefoil arches and the beautiful colonnaded peristyle have attained a wide reputation. Though in ruins, these temples speak eloquently of the glorious stone tradition of ancient Kashmir which continued till recent times. The versatility of Kashmir stone carvers is seen in the magnificent Caturanana, the four-faced Vishnu image preserved in the Sri Pratap Singh Museum, Srinagar. The master carvers of Kashmir transformed the textured details of bronze sculpture to stone. Stone work in the reign of Avantivarman (ninth century), and subsequent monarchs depicts how the master carver conveyed his sentiments through these masterpieces. Though well-versed in all elements of Indian iconography, the master carver created images like the Caturanana Vishnu which embodied various *vyuha* concepts depicting the boar and lion heads of Vishnu looking in four different directions and incorporating *bhu,* the earth goddess.

Mahesh-Murti; stone; ninth century; Akhnoor; Dogra Art Gallery, Jammu

The various aspects of the three-headed Shiva represent the benign face of Shiva at the centre flanked on either side by his ferocious aspect and the feminine face of his consort.

A marvel of the Mughal period is the embellished structure of black marble with fine carved pillars built by Shah Jehan at Shalimar Bagh in Srinagar. Mulla Akhoon's *madrassa* in the same city typifies Mughal architecture.

Stone carvers catered to the needs of various sections of Kashmiri society. Cooking bowls, ladles and other stone utensils surpass even the beauty of wheel-thrown earthern bowls. Cups and plates made from stone known as *sangi-nalwat* in shades of grey, yellow and green have pride of place in a Kashmiri kitchen. *Sangi-dalam* of Verinag is used by goldsmiths, while *sangi-baswatri* is used in medicine. The dressed stone *hamams* provide warmth during the winter months.

Stone choppers of the paleolithic period are reported to have come from Chakapalwal, Jammu. Superb stone images of Vishnu and Shiva from Akhnoor and the eighth century Shiva and Parvati masterpiece highlight the perfect skill the Jammu stone carver had attained. The beautiful carved stone horses — some larger than life-size — from Gul Gulabgarh and the stone *bowlies* are among the masterpieces created by the traditional stone carvers of the Jammu area. The superb temple clusters at Kiramchi and Babor provided the stone carver with an opportunity to display his exquisite workmanship in stone and are works of great beauty, dignity and serenity.

Far left

***Lungto*, stone cooking pot, early 20th century; Balistan, Ladakh**

Cooking at extremely high altitudes is a lengthy process and the heavy lid serves as a pressure cooker. Lamps, frying pans, griddles and *chhang* pots in stone were earlier supplied via Nubra from a village named Thukmus near Siksa.

***Zeharmora* pot, Srinagar, Kashmir**

Serpentine stone contains manganese oxide and ferrous which are believed to assist in the curing of many ailments. Cups, tumblers, kettles, jugs and bowls of serpentine were therefore made by artisans for both medicinal and utilitarian purposes. These were widely used in Jammu, Kashmir and Ladakh until recent times, when serpentine became rare and consequently prohibitively expensive.

Ornaments

In the early hymns of the Rig Veda, Indra, the most popular deity, is said to be the possessor of *ratna*, or jewellery. Panini's grammatical treatise, the *Ashtadhyayi* of the fifth century B.C., includes a number of ornaments which still retain their original names. Thus, from time immemorial, people have adorned themselves with precious ornaments and the people of Jammu, Kashmir and Ladakh vividly demonstrate the continuity of this tradition. The love of ornamentation and the skill with which stones, gold, silver and other materials were shaped to fashion jewellery show the remarkable imagination and dexterity of the craftspeople of this region.

The excavations of Burzahom yielded evidence of the use of square, rectangular and cylindrical beads made out of various precious stones such as agate and cornelian. Nineteen gold beads were also found in the later stages of the Burzahom settlement.

While the historian Kalhana in his *Rajatarangini* often refers to the *nupura hara*, anklet, *kankana*, wristlet, *keyura*, armlet, *parihara*, bracelet and *kundala*, earring; archaeological evidence all over

the state reveals the wealth of ornaments popular at different periods. At Manda near Akhnoor in Jammu the find of a double-headed, metallic hair-pin fashioned on the Harappan design speaks eloquently of the beautification of the female coiffure. An image of the first century A.D. found in Semthan, Bijbehara shows that women used to wear the *channavira* or cross-belt while men fancied ornamental caps. During the second and third century A.D. a large number of ornaments were used for embellishment and the people were so fond of them that they even used bejewelled trappings for their horses. Men and women wore huge circular *kundalas*, or earrings, which they continue to do in the rural areas of the state. Women wore large anklets, *nupura*, which continued till the eighth and ninth century A.D. and are used even today in the Jammu area. A golden hairpin-like ornament for the forehead, probably a symbol of marriage, is seen on the tiles found at Harwan in Kashmir and this tradition continues till today.

Besides the *surpa kundala* and *surpa hara*, snake-like ornaments, the fifth century A.D. stone masterpiece, Sadasiva, the highest and most comprehensive aspect of Shiva, from Fatehgarh, Baramulla, wears a small ornament near the cartilage of the ear. A similar ornament is worn by a devotee worshipping two Buddhist deities, Avalokiteshwara and Maitreya, painted on the famous wooden book covers from Gilgit (seventh century A.D.) of the six birch bark manuscripts found in 1931 and preserved at the Central Asian Museum in Srinagar. The ornament depicted has reappeared in recent years as part of modern fashion. Kalhana often refers to different crowns like the peaked tiara and the three crescent-mooned crown worn by kings and noblemen of ancient Kashmir. Sculptural evidence of the sixth century when a small crown is first seen, substantiates his statement and women of the Rajouri area in Jammu continue to wear a unique metallic cap or crown known as *chaunk phool*. During the sixth and seventh century A.D., a large ornamental and beaded necklace and heavy anklets were popular with both the men and women of Kashmir. Women wore silver and gold caps, with ear ornaments suspended from both sides and covered with a cloth. This was similar to the *chaunk phool* of Jammu. The *taj*, a small crown of silver or gold, fashioned like a peaked tiara, is still worn in urban Kashmir and is used by brides at the time of their marriage.

Previous page

Samanya Svadhinapatika, Basohli miniature painting, Dogra Art Gallery, Jammu

The *nayaka* and *nayaki*, the hero and heroine of love, are depicted in various moods, emotions and situations in a series of miniatures illustrating *Rasamanjari* or the Garland of Emotions, painted for Raja Kirpal Pal of Basohli between 1675 and 1695. The profusion of jewellery worn by all the figures is minutely and intricately created with shiny beetle wings and embossed effects to give the ornaments a three-dimensional aspect.

Far left

Bridal ornaments, Jammu

The *tika* on the forehead and the large nose ring, *balu*, are mandatory for a bride. The *balu* is supported by a chain extending up to the hair. Diamonds and pearls are set in gold with two ornamental peacocks balancing on the lower arc. Hollow gold beads strung together form a necklace, *kaintha*, while the partially visible *jhumkas*, earrings, are a combination of gold with emerald and ruby beads.

Centre

Ordali, a gold pendant with a serpentine stone on the reverse side, Jammu

The serpentine, locally called *zeharmora*, is a pale green stone which is said to guard against chest and heart diseases. The word literally means "the removal of poison". When set in a gold pendant with floral and bird motifs, it plays the part of a decorative talisman, particularly for the elderly.

Gold *band*, Jammu

This typically traditional wrist ornament in fine filigree is made by goldsmiths for bridal wear. Fitted with a clasp that opens to fit around the wrist, it is more like a bracelet than a bangle and is usually worn along with other gold and glass bangles.

Goldsmith at Fateh Kadal, Srinagar, Kashmir

In the heart of the old city of Srinagar, jewellery is still fashioned according to traditional requirements. To join finely worked sections of a silver bracelet, a goldsmith blows air through a thin pipe, directing a tongue of flame to the required spot.

Far right

***Halqaband*, ornament for the neck, brass, Kashmir**

Made in both silver and gold and, occasionally, in brass, the *halqaband* consists of a series of interlocking sections joined together with thread. It is studded with rubies, emeralds, semi-precious stones and sometimes even mirrors and is worn closely fitted against the throat.

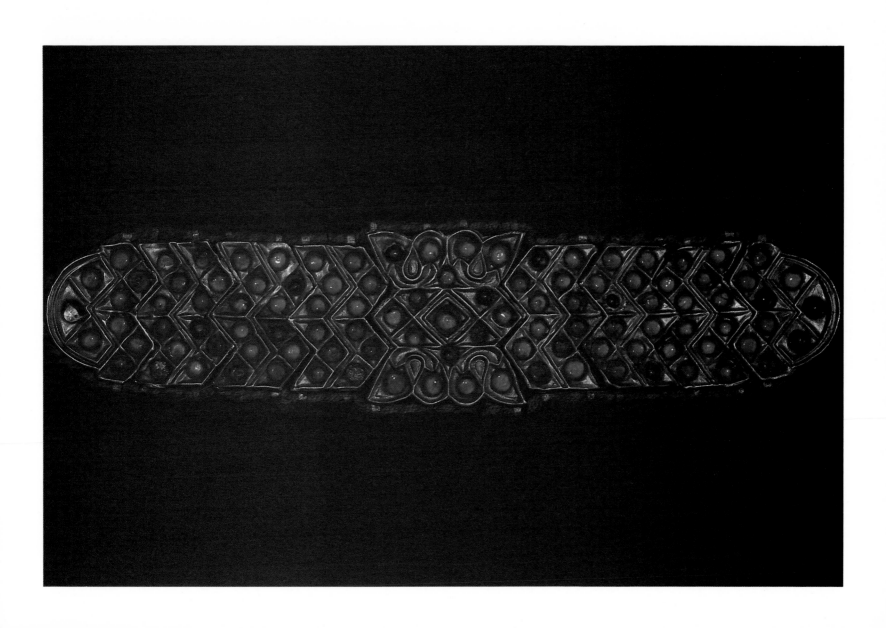

Armlets of many kinds, including bands of pearls, continued till Dogra rule in the 19th century when the *bazoband* became an important item of popular jewellery. The distinguishing features of this armlet were the stones set in gold or brass and strung together on a broad band of cloth with tasselled strings to hold them in place.

Long ear perforations and elongated ear lobes fitted with ear ornaments were a common feature of seventh century Kashmir. The fashion of wearing ornamental wristlets, rings and a huge necklace covering both shoulders is confirmed by the discovery in 1984 of a rare ninth century image of Vaikuntha at Anantnag. Vaikuntha is an image of a four-headed Vishnu representing his four manifestations as Vasudeva, Varaha, Narasimha and Kapil. This image, in which four manifestations of Vishnu are collectively represented in one body, was developed in Kashmir and is also known as Caturananan Vishnu. An ornamental *bayi* or wristlet seems to have been a favourite item among women of that time and continues to be popular in Kashmir. A seventh century stone sculpture from Pandrethan in Kashmir showing Siddhartha's birth depicts his mother Maya Devi wearing such an ornament as well as a beaded necklace similar in form to those worn by Ladakhi women today. The *bayi* is also given to Parvati in the ninth century composite image of Shiva and Parvati, commonly known as Ardhanarishvara, from Avantipur. Both these images are preserved in the Sri Pratap Singh Museum in Srinagar.

In the eighth century A.D. the *mekhala*, a girdle of various kinds, some with tinkling bells, became a favourite item and an image of Durga of the same period at the Sri Pratap Singh Museum, Srinagar, testifies to its popularity. When the two halves of the two deities are composed in one figure the characteristics of each are delineated through their jewellery, dress and coiffure. Master sculptors of Kashmir succeeded in depicting such individual characteristics of Harihara, an eighth century image representing both Shiva and Vishnu and which can be seen at the Berlin Museum; Ardhanarishvara, the ninth century androgynous man-woman figure which signifies the non-duality of divine nature found at Avantipur and Vishnu Kamalaja, the androgynous image of Vishnu with his consort Lakshmi. A profusion of ornaments was in vogue during the ninth century A.D., when King Avantivarman ruled over Kashmir and its adjoining areas.

Rural *halqaband*, Kashmir

A wide range of jewellery in white metal and brass was made for the rural population. Borrowing from traditional Kashmiri designs as well as from the nomadic tribes, they are richly ornamental at low cost.

White metal bands are welded to form sections joined together with coloured string. Bright foil in reds, greens, blues and gold is often placed under glass to create the effect of precious stones. Occasionally, paper from old cigarette packets is also used.

The *halqaband*, a neck ornament, appeared as an additional item of jewellery for women of this region during the eighth and ninth century, as a fragment of the Vaishnavi Lakshmi (Lakshmi as Vishnu's consort holding the conch, wheel, mace and lotus) at the Baroda Museum in Gujarat depicts. This ornament found its way into folkfore and poetry and remains an essential ornament for rural Kashmiri women.

The eighth century also saw the introduction of gems and ornaments on costumes. A beautiful eighth century sculpture from Kashmir at the National Museum, New Delhi, of Sasthi (the sustainer of the three worlds) with six sons of Kritas (Kartikeya, son of Shiva and Parvati) shows some of these figures in robes with small tinkling bells fixed on the lower edges of their costumes. The fact that this type of ornamented costume was worn till the middle of the 20th century is reflected in a verse by the contemporary poet Rehman Rahi: *"Shroni yeli boosum roni damnus, adeh nasa roodham panus tani"* (When I heard the jingle of her gown bedecked with tinkling bells on the edges, I could barely contain myself).

Queen Didda who ruled Kashmir during the 10th century introduced new styles into the dress and jewellery of this area. As a number of available bronzes of the period reveal, a cross belt worn by Kashmiri women in an earlier period reappears at this time for men.

The tenth century figures of the Bodhisattava; a fine wooden image of Tara, the benevolent goddess of Buddhism; Vasundhara, the earth goddess; and the eighth century stone figure of Avalokiteshwara, an attendant of Buddha, all found at the Alchi monastery in Ladakh provide proof of the variety of ornaments fashioned after Persian, Tibetan, Kashmiri and Central Asian traditions. Most of the present day jewellery used by men and women in Ladakh points to their continuity.

Jewellery received further enrichment in the Sultanate period which began in 1339 when gold, silver and precious stones were in demand for embellishing the body. Many new items, particularly the *tawiz* or amulet of different shapes, appear. These amulets continue to be worn as protection against evil influences or unlucky planets. Made with various gems including cats' eyes, sapphires, pearls, corals, and emeralds of different shapes, they held a written talisman inside and were attached to the *takani*, necklace and armlets, be-

Left

Chaunk phool, Jammu

A unique silver ornament worn on the head under the veil.

Right

Panjeb, silver anklets set with uncut emeralds, Jammu

Far left

Kana-vaji, a bunch of silver earrings, Bandipur, Kashmir

Suspended from the head with black thread or silver chains to support the weight, *kana-vaji* are now only worn by the elderly in rural areas.

Centre

Balti earrings, silver alloy, Kargil, Ladakh

The half-moon shape with filigree patterns is the most popular design worn by Balti women. The suspended tassels with tiny bells at the end are optional.

Balti peasant woman with silver earrings and metal head band, Dras, Ladakh

The Baltis belong to an old Indo-Aryan tribe which was converted to Shiite Islam from Buddhism in the 16th century. They live in Western Ladakh. The large circular silver earrings have adopted characteristics of the *kana-vaji* of Kashmir and the metal head-band is also a Kashmiri innovation. The hair-style remains typical of the Baltis.

coming an important constituent of women's jewellery.

Lapidaries known as *hakak* imported precious stones from Badakhshan, Bukhara and Yarkand via Ladakh but certain local stones are now frequently used. Jade was procured from Yarkand and used for pendants and is now obtained from the Paddar mines in the Kishtwar area.

The annexation of Kashmir to the Mughal empire gave a fillip to the jewellery of this area and the Empress Noor Jahan is said to have introduced a number of new ornaments, shapes and designs. Heavy jewellery in the form of necklaces, bracelets and the *tika*, a jewelled ornament for the forehead, reappears again during this period. Gold and silver buttons connected by a chain, were worn by the rich and are still used by many people in this region, including the nomadic Gujjars and Bakarwals.

The Dogra period in the mid-19th century introduced an element of the Pahari School of painting to the existing motifs and shapes of Kashmiri jewellery. The Pahari and Basohli painters of the 17th century laid great emphasis on the personal embellishment of the central male and female personages, the *nayaka* and *nayaki*, and it seems likely that they were well-versed in the techniques employed by gold and silversmiths as they provided three-dimensional jewellery to two-dimensional paintings for which they are famous throughout the world. Some of the royal scenes show men and women profusely bedecked with jewellery of pearls, gold and other precious metals. The figure of Krishna is shown wearing ornaments and in a number of paintings the *nayaki* is absorbed in adorning herself with ornaments. The Basohli painters used gold and silver paint extensively to heighten the effect of the shimmering ornaments and, as in some Rajasthani paintings, raised white paint was employed to depict pearls.

M.S. Randhawa, the noted art historian, writes in *Basohli Painting*: "Even demons are shown wearing necklaces. The crowns of gods and the necklaces, bracelets and earrings of women are decorated with beetle-wings cut into diamond-shaped pieces which greatly heighten the decorative effect of the paintings". While both the men and women of Jammu wore a considerable amount of jewellery until recently and the resplendent ornaments depicted in the Basohli School paintings reveal a rich heritage, today the uniqueness of style and design

is confined to a few pieces like the popular *panjeb* and the ceremonial *nath* or nose ring. This supposedly auspicious and ceremonial ornament covers the mouth and part of the cheek. Its weight is held up by a chain which is attached to the hair above the ears. The ring is often embellished with tiny figures of peacocks and parrots in precious stones set in gold. Changing circumstances and modern political systems have done away with occasions that support the daily use of expensive ornaments. Rural women in Jammu only wear silver anklets, the *chaunk phool*, bangles and the *tawiz* at weddings and village fairs.

In Jammu city, old and narrow winding lanes, such as the Jhulaka Mohalla, still house goldsmiths who repeat traditional designs of *jhumkas* and *naths* for local use. While every bride commissions a set of typically Dogri ornaments, designs from other parts of India are becoming popular for other social occasions. While men wore the *dastavana* or bangle and *goswara khanta* or earrings in the 19th century, today only Kashmiri women continue to adorn themselves with jewellery. Other ornaments typical and unique in this region are the *hunzura* which is used by newly-married brides to store *guli-meuth*, cash, given by relatives and friends. The *dejihor*, a symbol of marriage, is an old and unique ornament which is hung from the upper portion of the ears. It has attained almost religious sanctity and continues to be worn by almost every Pandit woman. *Gunus*, a thick bangle of solid gold and silver with a snake or lion-head at the two ends, has survived over the years.

In the valley, Srinagar has been the centre for the manufacture of both precious and semi-precious jewellery. In the vicinity of the Third Bridge, silver and gold leaf makers, copper workers, silversmiths and goldsmiths craft and sell traditional ornaments. A large part of their work is custom-made although some lower-priced *halqabands*, bracelets, hairclips and *tawiz*, in brass or white metal with glass or semi-precious stones, are made for sale to visiting rural folk. These craftsmen often buy old pieces of folk jewellery in exchange for a more modern piece of amorphous design. Bracelets engraved with the dial of a clock and broad square rings with route maps of mountain paths are among the treasures of these folk collections. An extraordinarily large and fascinating collection of rings, bracelets, shirt buttons, hair clips and bangles made brilliant with red and green foil placed

Far left

Drogpas or Brokpas, Ladakh

An exclusive and unique community of Dards who are said to be of pure Aryan stock live along the Indus between Skardu and Leh. The Baltis refer to them as "people of the mountain pastures". They are also called the people of Dahanu. Dard men and women wear long braids and bouffant trousers. They place the *molön khö*, a kind of folded sock, on their heads, stitched with charms, needles, buttons, amulets and coins. On top is pinned a large orange flower, *moon-thu-to*, which is first dried and then steamed so that it puffs up. *Tomar*, a silver medallion with long chains, hangs on the side of their foreheads.

Weaver's family, Mulbek, Ladakh

Mulbek, where Buddhist Ladakh begins, has a mixed population. Here, Shiite Muslims wear simpler ornamentation than the Buddhists. The circular brass ornaments worn on the shoulder are called *chapstey* from which tooth and ear picks may be suspended by a string. Old and worn coins attached to a chain of coral beads form a necklace, probably made by the weaver.

under glass are bought and sold by kilogram weight by local jewellers and traders.

Jewellery for personal ornamentation has been very popular in Ladakh, possibly because of royal patronage and its widespread use by the common people of the area. Worn by men and women, Ladakhi jewellery is unique and distinctive and bears the characteristics of its regional and historical links. The Balti peasant woman working in the fields between Dras and Kargil wears heavy and elaborate silver earrings, somewhat similar to her counterpart in Kashmir. Beyond Kargil, where the influence is Central Asian, turquoise, large and tiny pearls, coral, agate and cornelian dominate. Goldsmiths make fine filigree charm boxes and amulets while the women themselves string stones together to make simple necklaces.

The *perak* of Ladakh is undoubtedly the most extraordinary head dress in use anywhere in the world today. The grandeur of the head dress lies in the laying of any number from 20 to 200 large turquoise and other stones across a wide leather piece. The *perak* begins below the forehead, goes over the head and extends down the wearer's back to below waist level and is evocative of lizard scales, fins and a serpent's hood. This bejewelled hat recalls the legendary belief of the Ladakhis that women are from the underworld of *lhu* which is inhabited by snakes, lizards and fish. The underground divinities are ascribed fertility powers, which perhaps explains the link with women.

Historical explanations of the *perak's* origin remain unclear. However, legend has it that one of the kings of this area took as his queen a woman from a neighbouring region where a similar head dress was worn. In deference to their queen the style was adopted by the citizens of Ladakh. The black sheepskin ear flaps which stick out like wings or fins were supposedly added when the queen had an ear ache. Following her, or perhaps by order, the others did the same and the *perak* assumed its whimsical appearance.

In Ladakh, both sexes wear earrings from an early age, with the men occasionally wearing only one. The men's earrings consist of one or two small stones strung with thread and are simpler than those worn by women. Women wear rings, *sirkop*, given to them by their mothers-in-law during the customary marriage ceremonies. The *tunglag* are wide conch bangles worn on each wrist. The conch

Inset

Gahu, pendant in gold with turquoise and imitation red stones, Ladakh

Used as a charmbox, the *gahu* is worn suspended from a chain of pearls, with large turquoise and coral beads.

Detail of brooch, Leh, Ladakh

Silver or gold brooches and pendants are mounted with turquoise, coral, amber or imitation stones by *sergars*, goldsmiths. Brooches are worn attached to the shoulder.

Sergars work singly or in groups in tiny rooms sharing a common grate and the tools of their trade. Some goldsmiths in Leh are of Kashmiri origin but have become adept at making Ladakhi and Tibetan jewellery.

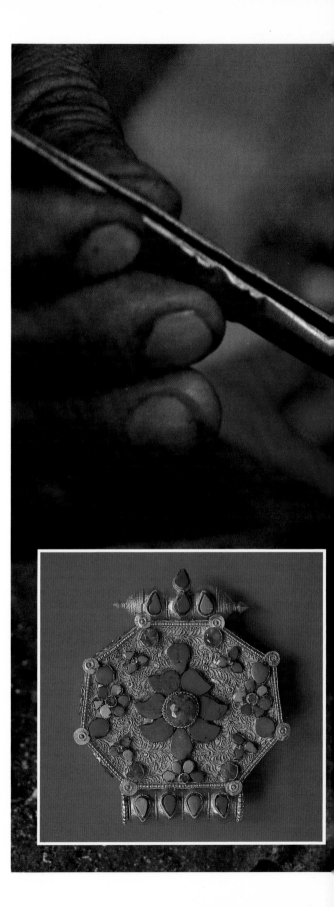

comes from Bengal and is fashioned into bangles by the *gara*. Sometimes they are studded with silver or dipped in colour. A mandatory item of ornamentation, the *tunglag* is worn by all women above 17 and are knocked against each other as a form of greeting. Simple metal bangles, *idugu*, with carved geometric designs, are also sometimes worn.

Like the *dejihor* worn in Kashmir by Pandit women, the Ladakhi woman wears an ornament called *sondus* or *branshil*, a marriage symbol fixed on the left shoulder. It consists of a few gold or silver discs connected by a number of long silver strands. This is given by a mother to her daughter at the time of her marriage. It is also functional as its lower portion is fitted with minute scoops and toothpicks to clean ear wax and teeth. The *sondus* is common in the Kashmir province as well as in urban areas of Ladakh and is worn on both shoulders. Another important ornament is the *bochah*, fitted near the left hip of women and shaped like the *sondus*. Ladakhi women also use neck ornaments, like the *halqaband*, called *sikaposh*, *multufchi* and *kanthi* and one finds these ornaments on those not wearing the *perak*.

To the west of Ladakh live descendants of an ancient Aryan tribe known as the Drogpas. Men, women and children of this tribe wear heavy metallic earrings through holes pierced in their earlobes. Irrespective of age and position, everyone wears long pigtails and covers their heads with caps and flowers. Drogpa marriage jewellery consists of rings and other ornaments made in silver by the village smith. Children wear caps with coloured stones, metallic jewellery, amulets and old coins very similar to those in Kashmir where these are fitted on the *takani* in urban areas. Men sometimes wear white earrings and they are fond of using white buttons as ear ornaments.

Wherever the folk tradition has survived in the state through geographic or cultural isolation, jewellery retaining ancient and symbolic designs is still worn in plenty and remains an important indication of beauty, wealth and status. In cities and towns, however, modernisation has often led to simplification and a moving away into a broader cosmopolitan framework where momentary fashion rather than symbolic or conventional values is satisfied. In spite of this, the skill of the artisan welding tiny silver bells to an anklet or adorning a bride for her wedding day continues to find an important place.

Far left

Ladakhi women wearing the *perak*, ornamental headdress, Leh, Ladakh

A Ladakhi woman's most prized possession, *perak* is worn not only on festive or ceremonial occasions but even ordinarily if she so wishes. It is handed down from mother to daughter, or daughter-in-law. In the absence of any close female relation of the next generation it is given to the monastery.

Shaped like a serpent with a spread hood, the *perak* is a long piece of leather extending from the forehead down the back to waist level. A cloth is stretched over the leather and enormous uncut turquoise stones — of which the largest is placed at the forehead — along with coral, agate and cornelian are stitched on to it in one to seven rows. A queen may have nine rows. At the top of the head a filigree charm box in silver or gold and mounted with stones may be attached. Extending outwards from underneath are separate earlaps, *tsaru*, of black sheepskin, giving the appearance of fins. The more ornate *perak* has a silver strip covered with large corals attached to one side along the back. The entire headdress may weigh more than three kilograms and cost up to Rs.30,000

Girl with ornaments, Leh, Ladakh

While pendants containing religious charms and brooches are made by *sergars*, the majority of women make their own necklaces, bracelets and even earrings.

Tiny seed pearls, *murik*, with turquoise, *yu*, coral, *churu*, and amber, *fi*, are the most popular and are bought in the Leh bazaar by weight, a *tola* measuring about eleven grams. The stones are not of local origin and their use has probably been influenced by the early traders between Persia and Central Asia.

Nam chokali, earrings, are worn by both sexes and supported by a thread which passes around the earlobe. Earlier, it was considered an essential form of ornamentation. Necklaces with large uncut coral and turquoise stones are worn on festive occasions. For everyday wear, smaller stones suffice.

Glossary

Acchi-dar: Lattice window

Aftaba: Water-pot

Ajrakh: Form of hand block printing common to Sind in Pakistan and Gujarat in India

Amli, amlikar: Embroidered; embroidered shawl from Kashmir

Angus: Cutter

Anna: One-sixteenth of a rupee (an old coin)

Ankoonan: Tool for engraving flower designs

Arama: Also known as *avasa*; early form of monastery made of brick as opposed to the earliest temporary shelter known as *vassavasa*

Ari: Small hooked awl used by embroiderers

Ashta-dala-padma: An eight-petalled lotus

Astar: Lining

Badam-gar: "Almond" design in *kani* work

Bahat: Kashmiri cargo boat

Baltoi: Vessel to cook *dal*

Balu: Nose ring

Bangala: "Related to Bengal" or "like the type that came from Bengal". The name for a house-boat that became popular after the Mughal emperor Akbar introduced the Bengal pattern in Kashmir. The name lingered till the end of the 19th century and is also used for a square tower constructed on the roof of a house.

Bati chalan: Rice spoon

Basta: Sheepskin bellows

Bayi: Wristlet

Bazaar: Marketplace

Behak: High mountain meadow

Bazoband: Armlet

Bhu: Earth goddess

Booni: Traditional Kashmiri name for *chinar*

Bindoo: Central point or dot

Boteh-meiri: Princely flower

Boteh: Term used for the cone which is woven or embroidered on Kashmir shawls, literally meaning flowers

Bowlies: Water tank with profusely carved walls

Brandisher: Polishing tool

Bulbul: Otocompsa *Molpastes leucogenys*

Bushkab: Eating bowl

Caturanana: Four-faced figure

Chadar: Blanket

Chals: Bird

Chand-dar: Moon design of *kani* shawls

Chhat: Sack made of goat's hair

Chhali: Goat's wool blanket hand-woven in Kargil, Ladakh

Chhang: Barley beer

Chhos-khor: Prayer wheel

Charkha: Spinning wheel

Chasmak kawal: Instrument to draw round flowers

Chashm-bulbul: One of the designs of Gurez *chadars* — small checks shaped like the eye of the *bulbul*

Chamcha: Spoon

Chaptsey: Circular brass ornament from Ladakh

Charakgar: Cleaner

Channavira: Cross belt

Chaunk phool: Silver ornament worn on the head under the veil

Cheet-misri: Egyptian design in *kani* work

Chikni: Style of embroidery

Chikri: Local Kashmiri name for *Buxux semperuirens*, prized for its smoothness and light colour

Chillum: Upper part of the hubble bubble containing tobacco

Chinar: Persian name for *Platanus orientalis*

Chipra: Head cloth or veil

Chipkiang: *Phragmites Communis* grass growing beside the Indus river in Ladakh

Chikandozi: The minute satin stitch used for small motifs

Choktsey: Local name for a small, low table with carved legs and sides, commonly made in Ladakh

Choga: Regal gown embroidered with golden/silver thread

Choncha: Ladle

Chot: Plain

Chot-wol: Maker of a plain object

Churu: Coral

Chya tsering: An auspicious figure

Coolie: Pack porter

Dal: Lentils

Dastavana: Bracelet; glove

Deg: Cooking vessel

Dejihor: Marriage ornament suspended on chain or thread from the hair and worn forward like earrings Hindu women of upper caste in Kashmir

Dembnao: Type of small dug-out boat manufactured in Kashmir. Used traditionally as a market boat selling vegetables and other essentials

Deodar: *Cedrus ibani, var. deodora*

Dhera: Caravan

Dhoopa-zoor: Clay incense burner

Dokkur: Hammer

Dorjay: A sceptre signifying a thunderbolt

Dosooti: Heavy cotton cloth for curtains and furnishings. "Do" means two and "sooti" is yarn. This yarn is double twisted.

Do-shala: Shawls in pairs. They are sometimes stitched together and embroidered.

Do-rukhi: Reversible shawl with embroidered outlines or borders

Draj: T-shaped iron object

Druk: Dragon

Druk khabrel: Decorative design with two dragons facing each other

Dug: Umbrella or canopy

Duldo: Silver necklace worn by Bakarwal women

Dungri: Small pot

Dunga: Common passenger boat of Kashmir, about 20 metres long and two metres wide

Dunli: Nose ring worn by Bakarwal women

Farsi baff: Pile as in Persian carpet

Farsh tram: Large round plate

Fi: Amber

Fruk pattu: See *pattu*

Gabba: Floor rug made from old blankets, waste wool or tattered woollens

Gagar: Vessel to store water

Gahu: Pendant in gold with turquoise and imitation red stones

Gara: Community of blacksmiths

Garwan: Clay pot for melting metal

Gaz: Measure of length fractionally over a yard

Geluga: Yellow sect of the lamas in Tibetan Buddhism

Ghee: Clarified butter

Goncha: Gown made of hand-woven or velvet cloth worn by Ladakhis

Gonder: Tuft

Gota: Metallic ribbon used to decorate garments

Gosheper: Wooden hammer

Goswara: Earrings

Gud-gud: Onomatopoeic name of Ladakhi tea vessel

Gul-andar-gul: Name of the design meaning "rose-within-rose"

Gule-vilayat: "Foreign flower", famed perhaps due to the later introductions of rose motifs into the composition. This is an inter-twining tree-formation of rose and apple blossom stalks.

Gul-e-anar: Pomegranate blossom design in *kani* work

Guli-hena: Flower design in Kashmiri carpet

Gulmaut: Presents; literal meaning "kissing of hands"

Gunus: Solid gold or silver open bangle with snake or lion head at two ends

Gyanakchagri: Chinese wall design

Hajam: Community of barbers

Hakak: Seal cutter

Halqaband: Neck ornament

Hamam: Chamber heated by steam passing through pipes under the floor

Hangul: Kashmiri stag

Hansli: Neck ornament in a moulded shape

Hara: Necklace

Hathodi: Hammer

Hazara: "Thousand flowers", named because the composition is a compact conglomeration of almost all flowers commonly found in the Kashmir valley

Hundash: Forceps

Hunzura: Long necklace fitted with a box at the centre for receiving cash presents by a bride

Huqqa, hukka: Tobacco water-pipe; hubble-bubble

Ikat: Weaves in which the thread is dyed according to a specific design prior to being woven

Iran: Solid iron block

Isbandsoz: Incense burner

Istea: A small fine hand-saw

Jai-nawaz: Prayer mat

Jamawar: Fabric length in *kani* weave

Janjeer: Chain

Jhumka: Hanging earring

Juma: Friday

Kaintha: Gold beaded necklace

Kakak: Lapidary work

Kalai: Application of tin foil

Kalam: Wooden implement used to trace a design on fabric, like a quill pen

Kalamdan: Pen holder

Kalami pattu: See *pattu*

Kalbaf: Carpet weaver

Kalbafi: Carpet weaving

Kandidar: Border of *chadars*

Kana-vaji: A bunch of silver earrings

Kangi: Comb

Kangri: Earthenware fire pot covered with willow basketry

Kani: Eyeless wooden bobbins (also known as *tujis*) used instead of the shuttle in weaving. The patterned pashmina material of shawls and *jamawars*. Also used to refer to the work so done

Kanikar: Loom-woven shawl, twill-tapestry weave

Kankana: Wristlets

Kanta: Necklace

Karkhana: Workshop or factory

Karkhandar: Owner of a workshop or factory

Kartak: Ceremonial tea bowl

Kasaba, qasaba: Cloth for covering the hair, used by Muslim women

Kathi: Willow bush of Badarwah

Kathul: Present area of Kathileshwar on the left bank just above the Second Bridge, Srinagar. Kalhana's *Kashthila* which Bilhanoe praises as the area of learned Brahmins. The name is indicative of the area being the abode of woodcraft architecture

Katore: Small metal bowl

Kats: *Indigoferra heternatha*

Kayur: Non-oily variety of pine wood; *Pinus excelsa*

Kenz: Tiny clay rice bowl

Keyura: Armlet

Khandwao: *Kani* weaver

Khar: Smith

Kharav: Wooden sandals

Khatirast: Striped design in *kani* work where the base cloth or border consists of bright lines, narrow stripes or bands

Khatumband: Decorative wooden joinery

Khatwav: Rough iron file

Khos: Cup

Kilim: Patterned weave of Iran, West and Central Asia, achieved by a simpler mode of the *kani* technique. Flat-weave carpet or rug

Kiltu: Large basket

Kind: Large enclosure

Koll: Earthen grain container

Konda: Kiln

Konka: Small nose-ring worn by Bakarwals

Kotha: Flat-roofed homes of semi-permanent nomads

Kral: Potter

Kunda: Round bowl

Kundala: Earring

Kurkot: A piece of over-heated and solidified lava-like chunk of clay collected from the abandoned kilns of red-clay potters. These pieces, after smoothening one of the surfaces, are used in the preparation of papier-maché objects

Kurta: Knee-length shirt worn by men and women

Kutkol: Canal

Kyu-posh: Floral design in *kani* work

La: Pass

Lachka: Embroidered Bakarwal cap

Laong: Nose-ring worn by nomad women in the Jammu region

Ldugu: Metal bangle worn by Ladakhi women

Leij: Earthen cooking pot

Lena: General name for Buddhist monastery built of stone and brick

Loi: Blankets usually made of handspun wool, woven by families for their own use in villages

Lokpa: Ladakhi garment worn by women to cover their backs

Longure: Rice measure

Lota: Mug with lid

Lui: *Cotoneaster*

Lungi: Waist-cloth

Lungto: Stone cooking pot

Madrasa: Theological school of the medieval period

Maitreya: Future Buddha

Makara: Water demon from Buddhist mythology

Majma: Large platter

Malchang: Willow

Manah: Terracotta container

Mani: Walls of stones piled together, many of which have carved inscriptions

Mandala: Circles in religious art

Mantra: Series of sacred sounds; as part of Hindu and Buddhist ritual a *mantra* is repeated either in silence or aloud, to aid concentration during meditation

Martaban: Glazed container for pickles

Masnad: Floor covering made of hand-woven and hand-printed cotton cloth

Math: Large earthen jar

Mattah: Main body of a papier maché object

Mehrab: Archway

Mekh: Large iron rod

Mendiyari: Braided hair-style of nomads

Mekhala: Girdle

Mentok: Floral

Mochi: Cobbler

Mohalla: Section of a town

Mölon khö: Dard cap

Moraskar: Knot stitch, invariably used with metallic thread in Kashmir for gowns and shawls

Mun-thu-to: Red flower worn on caps by Dards

Murik: Tiny seed pearls

Naga: Serpent, cobra

Nala: A spatula resembling a painting knife

Namchokali: Earrings

Namda: Carpet made out of wool and cotton pressed together and embroidered in chain stitch

Naqash: Pattern-maker, pattern-drawer in *kani* work. Engraver in metalwork

Nayaka: Male

Nayaki: Female

Neela-thota: Copper sulphate

Nukta: Harness straps made of goat's hair by nomads

Numdah: Felt carpet

Nupura: Anklet

Nyingmapa: Red Sect of Lamas in Tibetan Buddhism

Odhni: Head-cloth or veil

Ordali: Pendant

Padma: Lotus blossom

Paila Nor: Cup, container

Palpyu: Geometric "lucky" designs of the pre-Buddhist Bönpa religion

Pandits: Teachers and priests of the Brahmin community

Panjeb: Anklets

Parandi: Hair-tie made of black cotton threads with decorative tassels

Parinda: Type of swift-moving Kashmiri boat seating four passengers and steered by 40 to 50 paddlers

Parihara: Bracelet

Parwa: Miniature earthen plate

Pashm: Warm, soft, winter under-fleece of a trans-Himalayan breed of the domestic goat, the raw material of the best *kani* work

Pashmina: Yarn spun and the cloth woven from goat's fleece from the Persian word pashm, wool. Name for Kashmiri shawl cloth

Patila: Deep bowl

Pattu: Tweed-like woollen material woven in the hill areas of Jammu and Kashmir state. *Kalami pattu,* superfine variety of *pattu* formerly produced at Sopore. *Fruk pattu,* the *pattu* produced in Ladakh

Perak: Ornamental turquoise-studded Ladakhi head-dress for women

Pheran: Knee or mid-calf length gown worn by men and women in Kashmir

Pherba, tsokthal: Goats' wool blanket hand-woven in Ladakh

Phukstel: Large pack basket made of grass

Phulkari: An embroidery form of the Punjab

Pie: $1/64$th of a rupee (old coin)

Pinjara: Cage. A complex form of wood craft in which lattices of thin intersecting slats of wood are built

Pits: Reed mace, *Typha sp.* a swamp plant

Poshkani: *Parrotia Jacquenontiana*

Poshkar: "Flower-bouquet" design in *kani* work

Posh mech: Flower dust

Prabhavali: Halo of an image

Pritz: Large reel used for winding yarn in pashmina spinning

Pulahru: Straw shoes

Pumpa: Holy vase

Punj pehlu: Design in wooden lattice work

Punja dar: "Five-petalled flower" design in *kani* work

Qasaba: Square shawl in *kani* pashmina for women's wear. Also called *rumal*

Raffal: Worsted or machine-spun wool obtained from merino sheep

Raffoogar: Darner, embroiderer, needleman

Rawa: One of the designs of Gurez *chadars* — large multiple checks

Razdani: Usually the word means capital city, but in Kashmiri the word is specifically used for the king's palace. The famous palace that Zain-ul-Abadin built was also known as Razdani

Resham: Silk

Roshangar: Polisher

Rumal: Square shawl, kerchief

Sadak: Religious savants

Sadhana: Meditation

Sagla: Vessel to cook rice

Sakhtasazi: Building or evolving the basic shape

Samawar, samovar: Tea kettle

Saniwar: Small vessel

Sanzi-war: Vanity box

Sar: To prepare

Sarpa-hara: Snake-shaped necklace

Sarpa-kundala: Snake-shaped earring

Seeli: Rope tied around horse's neck

Sergar: Silversmith, goldsmith

Seumba: Instrument used for engraving a deep design

Shabi-chirag: Night lamp

Shagird: Apprentice

Shah-pasand: Royal choice design of *kani* shawl

Shah-tus: Fine and expensive wool obtained from mountain goats reared at high altitudes

Shaksaz: Basket maker

Shakstar: Ladkahi floor matting woven out of chipkiang grass

Shamiana: Gay tent pitched in the open; printed or embroidered, it was generally used for state functions in summer

Shamla: Waist-girdle in *kani* work

Sharanz: Forcep

Sheekh: Iron rod

Shawl-tarah: Shawl pattern

Shikara: Boat paddled by one or more oarsman on the lakes of Kashmir

Shikargah: Shawl embellished with a hunting scene

Shushur: Frost

Sofyanarang: General concept of colour which lays emphasis on pastel shades, preferably fabrics with white background

Sondus: Ornament worn on the left shoulder by married women in Ladakh

Soni poutul: A miniature earthen *linga*

Soof: Coarse cloth

Sozani, sozankar: "Sozan" is needle, "kar" is work. Hence, needlework done on shawls. The embroiderer who outlines the *kani* design on shawls

Sri-chakra: Graphic symbolism of the stages of meditation

Sun tram: Deep plate

Surahi: Long-necked flask

Suttan: Loosely gathered pyjama

Takani: Skull cap

Talim: Design coded in a sort of shorthand (used in carpet, *kani* shawl weaving)

Talim-guru: pattern writer in *kani* work

Tarah-guru: Pattern-colourer in *kani* work

Taranga: Band used by Hindu women to tie their hair

Tashistatz gyat: Combination of eight lucky signs of Buddhist iconography

Tashnar: Water jug and basin

Tashwan: Refers to the area between the river Vitasta and the Kutkol canal. This area was a dense forest that beautified the landscape, therefore the name Tashwan. The name still refers to an area that lies between the Third Bridge (Fateh Kadal) and the Fourth Bridge (Zaina Kadal) on the left bank of the river

Tawiz: Amulet

Thaj: Pot made of iron for melting copper

Thankha: Religious scroll

Thap chabrik: Iron stove

Teliwar: Oil container

Tibi: Hat worn by Ladakhi men and women

Tika: Forehead ornament

Tikli: Hand-spindle

Tilla: Embroidery work using gold and silver thread

Tilo: Small nose-ring worn by Bakarwal women

Tola: Measure of weight, approx 11 gms.

Tomar: Silver medallion

Toor: Bowl

Toshakhana: Store of state treasures

Trangdi: Rope netting

Tsapli: Straw sandal

Tsaru: Sheepskin

Tsepo: Small pack basket made of *chipkiang* in Ladakh

Tsod: Vase

Tsot: Local name in Ladakh for a wild plant used for making maroon dye

Tsukdan: Ceremonial Ladakhi carpet

Tunglag: Conch bangles worn by Ladakhi women

Tus: Pashm of certain goat-like wild animals, especially the chiru and perhaps also the ibex

Ustad: Master craftsman, usually a teacher

Vaar: Resting place or residence

Vajra: Holy instrument; sceptre

Vassavasa: Earliest form of resting place for Buddhist monks. These were very basic temporary rain shelters to which monks would retreat during the monsoon season. The *vassavasa* was the forerunner of the Buddhist monastery

Vasta: Head craftsman

Vata-chikan: Buttonhole stitch used to fill large spaces

Vihar: Resting place or residing place

Vyuha: Emanatory form

Waar: Small vase

Waggu: Reed matting

Wani: Community of small traders

Wor: Resting place or residence

Yandrewah: Horizontal iron plate with different sized holes for making wire

Yender: Kashmiri spinning-wheel

Yember-zal: Narcissus; floral pattern

Yu: Turquoise

Yogi: Religious teacher

Yumdumlagyut: Prayer-room decoration

Zaina-dub: In Kashmiri "dub" means balcony. Refers to that high portion of a great balcony that formed the topmost part of the 12th storey of Zain-ul-Abadin's palace

Zal: Chain

Zalakdozi: Chain stitch, a commonly used stitch for a variety of fabrics

Zali-pinjara: Lattice-window

Zama: Mud vessel to store *chhang*

Zang: Copper

Zanjeer: Narrow border of shawl or *chadar*

Zarcob: Gilder

Zari: Gold or silver thread used in embroidery/weaving

Zeharmora: Serpentine stone

Ziarat: Shrine

Zo, zomo: Breed of cattle in Ladakh evolved by crossing the cow with the yak

Bibliography

Ahad, Abdul. *Kashmir to Frankfurt: A Study in Arts and Crafts.* New Delhi, 1987.

Ames, Frank. *The Kashmir Shawl and its Indo-French Influence.* Woodbridge, UK, 1986.

Anon. Why Paisley? Paisley, U.K., 1985.

Azad, Maulvi Mohammed Hussain. *Darbare-Akbari* (Persian).

Bamzai, P.N.K. *A History of Kashmir — Political, Social and Cultural.* 2nd Edition, New Delhi, 1973.

Barker, Alfred F. *The Cottage Textile Industries of Kashmir and their Prospective Development.* Leeds, UK, 1933.

Bates, C.E. *A Gazetteer of Kashmir and the Adjacent Districts.* Calcutta, 1873.

Bernier, Francois. *Travels in the Moghul Empire 1656-1668,* 2 Vols., translation, A. Constable, Westminister, U.K. 1891.

Bilhana, Mahakavi. *Vikramankadeva Charitam.* Sarva XIII. Sanskrit Sahitya Research Committee of Benaras Hindu University. 1964

Birdwood, Sir George. *Industrial Arts of India,* London, Chapman & Hill Limited, London, UK, 1880.

Brijbhushan, Jamila. *Masterpieces of Indian Jewellery,* Delhi, 1975.

Chandra, Moti. *Costumes, Textiles, Cosmetics and Coiffure in Ancient and Medieval India.* Delhi, 1973.

Charak, S.S. *History and Culture of Himalayan States,* Vol. V, Part-II. Light and Life Publishers, New Delhi, 1980.

Chattopadhyaya, Kamaladevi. *Handicrafts of India.* Indraprastha Press, 2nd Edition, Delhi, 1985.

Chattopadhyaya, Kamaladevi. *Indian Carpets and Floor Coverings.* All India Handicrafts Board, Delhi, 1966.

Clabburn, Pamela. *Shawls.* Aylesbury, UK, 1981.

Cunningham, Alexander. *Ladakh.* Sagar Publications, 1977 (reprint).

Curatola, Giovanni. *Oriental Carpets.* Souvenir Press Ltd., London, 1983.

Fazl, Abul. *Ain-i-Akbari.* 2 Vols., translation H. Blochmann, 2nd edition revised D.C. Phillott, Calcutta, 1927.

Forster, George. *A Journey from Bengal to England.* London, 1798.

Hallade, Madeleine. *Gandhara Style and the Evolution of Buddhist Art.* Thames and Hudson, London.

Harrer Heinrich. *Ladakh.* Delhi, 1980.

Hassan Shah Sahibzada. *Tarikh-i-Hassan.* Srinagar, 1954.

Hope, Albrecht. *Oriental Carpets and Rugs.* Thames and Hudson, London, 1967.

Hugel, Baron Charles Von. *Kashmir under Maharaja Ranjit Singh.* Translation Jervis, London, 1845.

Hugel, Baron Charles Von. *Travels in Kashmir and the Punjab.* Translation Jervis, London, 1845.

Irwin, John. *The Kashmir Shawl.* London, 1973.

Jahangir, Emperor. *Tuzuk-i-Jahangiri.* 2 vols., translation, Alexander Rogers, ed. Henry Beveridge, London 1909, 1914.

Kak, R.C. *Ancient Monuments of Kashmir.*

Kango, G.H. and Dhar, B. *Studies in Transhumant Pastoralism in Northwest Himalayas Part-I.* Directorate of Soil Conservation, 1981.

Kaplanian, Patrick. *Les Ladakhi du Cashmire.* Hachette, 1981.

Khan, Mohammed Ishaq. *History of Srinagar, 1846-1947: A Study in Socio-Cultural Change.* Srinagar, 1978.

Khatana, R.P. *Gujjar, Gojri Zaban-ud-Adab.* (Urdu) Anjuman Tariqi Gojri, Haryana, 1974.

Khosla, Romi. *Buddhist Monasteries in the Western Himalayas.* Ratna Pustak Bhandar, Nepal, 1979.

Kosambi, D.D. *The Culture and Civilisation of Ancient India in Historical Outline.* Vikas Publishing House, New Delhi, 1972.

Kramrisch, Stella. *Manifestations of Shiva,* Philadelphia, 1981.

Kripa Ram Dewan. *Gulzar-i-Kashmir.* Lahore, 1870.

Lawrence, Walter. *The Valley of Kashmir.* Kesar Publishers, (reprint).

Mahakavi Bilhana. *Vikramankadeva Charitam. Sarva XVIII;* Sanskrit Sahitya Research Committee of Benares Hindu University, 1964.

Mitra, A. *The Arts and Industries in Kashmir.* Srinagar, 1912.

Moorcroft, William and Trebeck, George. *Travels in the Himalayan Provinces of Hindustan and the Punjab; in Ladakh and Kashmir; in Peshwar, Kabul, Kunduz and Bokhara.* Ed. H.H. Wilson, Sagar Publications, (reprint).

Pal, P. *Bronzes of Kashmir.* Graz, 1975.

Pandit, R.S. *Kalhan's Rajatarangani.* The Indian Press Limited, Allahabad, 1935.

Pandita, K.N. *Kashmir Shawl*. Srinagar, 1987.

Randhawa, M.S., *Basohli Paintings*. The Publications Division, Ministry of Information and Broadcasting, Govt. of India, 1959.

Rao, Gopinath T.N. *Elements of Hindu Iconography*. Vol. II, part II, Delhi, 1971.

Watt, George and Brown, Percy. *Arts and Crafts of India*. Cosmo Publications, 1979 (reprint).

Younghusband, Francis. *Kashmir*. A & C Black Ltd., London, 1933.

Zu Windisch Graetz, Stephanie & Christian. *Himalayan Kingdoms*. Roli Publications, Delhi, 1985.

Zwalf, W. *Heritage of Tibet*. Britain, 1981.

Ruedin, E. Gans. *Indian Carpets*, Thames & Hudson, London, 1987.

Saraf, D.N. *Arts and Crafts. Jammu & Kashmir*. Abhinav Publications, New Delhi, 1987.

Saraf, D.N. *Indian Crafts*. Vikas Publishing House, New Delhi, 1982.

Sharma, D.C. *Kashmir Under the Sikhs*. Delhi, 1983.

Singh, Gurcharan. *Pottery in India*. Delhi, 1979.

Singh, Madanjit. *Himalayan Art*. Macmillan, London, 1968.

Singh, Raghubir. *Kashmir*. Perennial Press, 1983.

Snellgrove, David & Skorupski, Tadens. *The Cultural Heritage of Ladakh*. Vikas Publishing House, New Delhi 1977.

Sufi, G.M.D. *Islamic Culture in Kashmir*. Light and Life Publications, New Delhi, 1979.

Sufi, G.M.D. *Kashmir — A History of Kashmir*, Vol. I, Lahore, University of Punjab, 1949.

Swarup, Shanti. *The Arts and Crafts of India and Pakistan*. D.B. Taraporewala Sons & Co. Ltd., 1957.

Swinburne, T.R. *Holiday in the Happy Valley*. Sagar Publications, New Delhi, 1970.

Uhlig, H. *Typen Der Bergbauern und Wanderhirten in Kaschmir und Jaumsar-Bawar*. Deustscher Geographentlag Koln, Franz Steiner Verlag GMBH - Weisbaden, West Germany.

Varadarajan, Lotika. *Kani Pashmina of Kashmir*. Ray, A. Sanyal, H. and Ray S.C. Eds. Indian Essays presented in memory of Professor Niharranjan Ray, Delhi, 1984.

Vigne, G.T. *Travels in Kashmir, Ladakh*. Iskardo, London, 1842.

Wadell, Austin. *Buddhism and Lamaism of Tibet*. Asian Publishers, (reprint) 1978.

Wakefield, W. *History of Kashmir and the Kashmiris*. London, 1879.

GAZETTEERS/PAPERS/MAGAZINES/JOURNALS

Adab, Zoon. Academy Publication, Srinagar, 1954.

Ahad, Abdul. "Muslim Karkhanas of Medieval Kashmir," in *Islam and the Muslim Age*, August, 1983.

Bhan, R.K. Economic Survey Report of Silverware in Kashmir, No.3, Srinagar, 1938.

Dattatreya, D. "The Gujars", article in *Kashmir*, February, 1955.

Irwin, John. "Arts and Crafts," *Marg*, Vol. VIII, March, 1955.

Kak, M.L. *Ladakh — A Land of Alluring Arts, Crafts*. Magazine of the Directorate of Handicrafts, Jammu and Kashmir, 1984.

Karpinski, Caroline. "Kashmir to Paisley". The Metropolitan Museum of Art Bulletin. New York, November 1963.

Lone, M. Gujjars and Bakerwals. Series of articles in *Nawa-i-Subh* weekly, August 30 to October 11, 1980.

Mikosch, Elizabeth. "The Scent of Flowers: Kashmir Shawls in the Collection of the Textile Museum." Textile Museum Journal, Washington DC. Vol.24, 1985.

Nazki, F. "Gujjars of Kashmir", articles in *New Delhi*, 3rd Edition, March, 1987.

Nichols, Marg. Mohammedan Architecture, *Marg*, Vol. VIII, March 1955.

Randhawa, M.S. & Premnath. Farmers of India, Vol. I. ICAR, New Delhi.

Rao, Aparna. & Casimir J. "Pastoral Niches in the Western Himalayas," *Himalayan Research Bulletin*, Vol. 5. No.1.

Wright, H.L. "Goat Grazing in Kashmir." *Indian Forester*, January 1932.

Gazetteer of Kashmir and Ladakh. First published in 1890 by the Superintendent of Government Printing, Calcutta, reprinted by Vivek Publishing House, Delhi, 1980.

"Carpets of India", article in *Marg*, Vol. XVIII No.4, September, 1965.

Information Digest on Jammu Handicrafts, M.E.C. Office of Development Commissioner. Jammu, 1986.

Research Biannual. Jammu & Kashmir Government, Vol. I, No.2, Srinagar, 1976.

Acknowledgements

The enthusiasm and remarkable co-operation shown by everyone even remotely concerned with the preparation of this book calls for gratitude that is difficult to express in words. The foremost acknowledgement, however, must go to the proud and skilled craftspeople of Jammu, Kashmir and Ladakh who patiently and cheerfully displayed their work with a great sense of pride yet humble detachment from the world of writers, publishers, editors and photographers! Among them, to name only a few, are Khazir Mohamad Kasba, Ghulam Mohamad Kanihama, Ishey Murup and Sonam Tsering. Friends displayed exquisite work commissioned, manufactured or retailed by them including Gulam Rassul and Mohamad Amin of Gulam Mohidin and Son, Afzal Abdullah of Asia Crafts, A.G. Khan of Noor Din Khan and Brothers, M/s Khajawal and Tsewang Tondup of Ladakh Art Palace.

The Sri Pratap Singh Museum at Srinagar and the Dogra Art Gallery at Jammu were kind enough to permit photography from their vast collection.

Friends were warm-hearted and freely threw open their doors so that we could study and photograph pieces from their private collections. Among them special thanks are due to Mr and Mrs Aman Wazir of Jammu, Rigzin Namgyal 'Kalon' and Tonyot Shah of Leh.

The Jammu and Kashmir Handicraft Sales and Export Corporation and the Directorate of Handicrafts of Jammu and Srinagar extended generous help. The Jammu Marketing Extension Centre, Office of the Development Commissioner for Handicrafts, Prof. P.N. Mago, who carried out a survey of the crafts of Kashmir in the early sixties, Dr. Mohamad Amin, Michael Henderson, Ghulam Ahmed Malik and the weavers employed in his workshop, Akbar Mir, M. Samoon and M.L. Sapru provided information and assistance.

The staff and master craftsmen of the School of Designs, Srinagar, the Jammu and Kashmir State Handloom Corporation and the State Wool Board were important links in a coordinated effort to reach the concerned craftspeople.

Biodata

Mohidin Shah and Bubli and Yusuf Khan helped both in their official and private capacity far beyond the call of duty.

George Fernandes, Mahendra and Vina Sabharwal, Dr. M.K. Magazine, Salim Beg, Tapan Bose and Dr. Jyotindra Jain gave invaluable help — both practical and academic. The unflagging enthusiasm and physical energy of Sonam Dorjay who accompanied us to Sabu, Likir, Alchi and Chushot in search of all manner of art, craft, grass and stone needs special acknowledgement. Mr. Batappa, Mr. Kakpori and Akbar Ladakhi provided excellent guidance. Many thanks to Ayesha Kagal for copy-editing the manuscript.

Srinivas was a persistently cheerful assistant and typist and Rajinder Newton aided in untangling considerable lengths of manuscript as did Aditi Jaitly who doubled as a competent photographer's aide.

Infinite patience and immeasurable boosts of morale from families and colleagues were ultimately responsible for transforming work into pleasure.

JANET RIZVI, freelance writer and historian, did her Ph.D. in Indian history from Cambridge. She lived for two years in Ladakh and is the author of *Ladakh, Crossroads of High Asia* (Oxford University Press, New Delhi, 1983). She writes on historical and environmental subjects, and her articles and reviews have appeared in *Development Forum* (United Nations), *Mountain Research and Development* (Boulder, Colorado), *The India International Centre Quarterly* (New Delhi), *The India Magazine* (New Delhi), *The Statesman* (Calcutta and New Delhi) and other Indian newspapers. She is at present engaged in research on the history of Ladakh, using the oral method.

SUSHIL WAKHLU is an engineer by profession who has a deep interest in culture, history and the arts. He has written for *The India Magazine* on "The Pandas of Mattan", a community of Brahmins who live in Kashmir. A similar study on "The Fishermen Community" has been completed. He has also written about Delhi — the old city — on its traditions and institutions which have survived till today. He is the author of a conservation report on the traditional monuments and customs of Kashmir. While he belongs to Kashmir, he lives and works outside the state.

D.N. SARAF belongs to Jammu and Kashmir. He graduated in commerce, did his M.A. in economics and took a special course in marketing at the Harvard Business School. He has been associated with the Indian Crafts Council, the American Marketing Association and the British Institute of Management.

Saraf started his professional career with the development of crafts in Jammu and Kashmir. He held several managerial positions before becoming Vice-Chairman, Central Cottage Industries Emporium; Member Secretary, All India Handicrafts Board; and retired as Development Commissioner for Handicrafts, Government of India. In his last government post, Saraf was responsible for introducing a large-scale carpet weaving training programme. He has also worked on several U.N. assignments

and is at present president of the Delhi Crafts Council.

Widely travelled and the author of several reports and papers, his publications include two books *Indian Crafts: Their Potential and Development* (1982, revised edition 1985) and *Arts and Crafts, Jammu and Kashmir* (1987).

P.N. KACHRU is an artist with a diploma in fine arts and commercial painting from the London Institute of Technology. He has been a founder member of several institutions concerned with art and culture, including the Natural Cultural Front (1947), the Progressive Artists' Association (1949), the Kashmir Art Society (1960), and the State Design Development Centre (School of Designs). Kachru has held several one-man shows and group exhibitions in Delhi, Bombay and Calcutta, has participated in a number of national art exhibitions and is the recipient of several awards for his paintings. He has written many surveys, reports and articles which include: "The Ushkar School Movement in Terracottas", "Kashmir Papier Maché: A Historical Perspective", "Samba Textile Prints", "The Medieval Architectural Woodworks and Woodcrafts of Kashmir", "Handicraft Survey of Jammu Province", "Bara Masa in Pahari Paintings", and "Kashmir Glazed Potteries". He lives in Srinagar, Kashmir.

RANJANA THAPALYAL is a sculptor who has specialised in ceramics at the West Surrey College of Art and Design in the U.K. She has participated in group exhibitions in London, at the Mall Gallery and the London College of Furniture. She displayed her work in the Exhibition of Indian Women Sculptors at the National Gallery of Modern Art, New Delhi, the VIth Triennale, India, and at the Bombay Arts Festival in November 1987. Her solo exhibitions have been held at art galleries in New Delhi, Madras and Bombay. She has done design work for a theatre company in Geneva and taught painting at schools in Delhi, including art therapy for the disabled. She has worked among the traditional potters of Delhi developing new designs.

Her writings include articles on ceramists, pottery and art and cultural identity for the *Art Heritage* catalogue, New Delhi, *Link* magazine and the Hindi journal *Dinman*.

GULAM HASSAN KANGO belongs to Kashmir and is a member of the Indian Forest Service. He has worked for many years in the Forest and Soil Conservation Department of the government of Jammu and Kashmir, travelling extensively in the forest and hill areas of the state. He developed a keen interest in the nomadic people and their lifestyle and has done pioneering work in the classification of nomadic routes. He has published a study titled "Transhumant Pastoralism in North-West Himalayas". Kango is presently Director of Soil Conservation in Jammu and Kashmir and has many research papers on conservation to his credit. He has participated in a number of national and international conferences on matters related to the environment.

J.L. BHAN was born in Srinagar. After completing his early education in Kashmir and obtaining a diploma in painting and decoration he went to Baroda where he secured a masters' degree in museology.

From 1964 to 1976 he worked as curator of the Sri Pratap Singh Museum, Srinagar. He documented thousands of antiquities relating to the art of Jammu, Kashmir and Ladakh in his capacity as Registering Officer, Antiquities, J & K State, till 1979. He was appointed lecturer-cum-curator, Centre of Central Asian Studies, University of Kashmir, Srinagar, where he established the first Area Studies Museum in India. He is presently working as Reader and Head of the Central Asian Museum, University of Kashmir.

Bhan has travelled widely in India and abroad, including the USSR, Central Asia and the United Kingdom. He is a member of various national and international organisations including the International Council of Museums, Paris; Museums Association of India and the Indian Association of Art Historians. Bhan has published many articles based on original research in national and international journals and is currently working on a catalogue of Kashmir sculpture and art for the forthcoming Macmillan's *Dictionary of Art*, London.

SUNITA KANVINDE did her post-graduation in graphics from London and worked for Paul Elek Publishers, London. She worked as a designer on "Aditi", a major exhibition at the Festival of India, London, in 1982 and was given the national award for design in the same year for the "Aditi" catalogue.

She has also participated in several group shows and has held a one-woman show at Art Heritage in Delhi. She is currently working as a freelance designer with different projects in hand, including graphics for a hospital in Nepal.

Captions

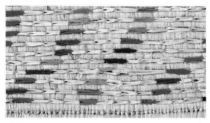

Endpaper

Detail of *jai* nawaz, prayer mat, wheat straw, Kishtwar, Jammu

Prayer mats have always played an important role in the life of the Muslim population. While carpets 80 cms × 80 cms are generally used, square mats woven in grass and wheat straw serve the rural people as floor mats on which to kneel for their daily prayers. Brightly coloured woollen threads add vibrance to the light golden hue of the wheat straw.

Page 4-5

Craftsman working on crewel or chain stitch embroidery near Anantnag, Kashmir

As the snows melt in the spring, craftsmen in rural areas sit beside streams to embroider lengths of *dosooti,* a handwoven fabric in double twisted yarn. The floral and geometric designs done in woollen thread with an awl convert the plain fabric into decorative furnishing cloth.

Page 1

Gujjar woman with embroidered *lachka*, Kashmir

The finely embroidered cap with embedded metallic pieces and red and yellow silk thread in fine chain stitch and a manner of cross stitch reflects the individual creativity of the wearer. Gujjar women fashion their hair into many tiny, well-oiled braids which do not have to be undone during long journeys. The heavy silver beads and *taveez,* amulets, were probably made by a jeweller at Rajouri.

Page 6-7

The Tawi river at Jammu

The river flows past the Bahu Fort which was the original capital of its founder King Jambulochan. The new city was built on the small ridges on the left bank of the river. The snows of the Pir Panjal divide Jammu from the valley of Kashmir.

Page 2-3

Balti family at work in the fields below Dras, Ladakh

Baltistan, where cultivated Ladakh begins, reflects influences of both Kashmir and Muslim Ladakh.

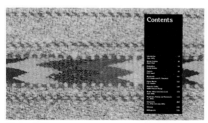

Page 8-9

Section of Bandipur *chadar*, Kashmir

Rough hand-spun and hand-woven shawls with a colourful *kani* border are worn by the rural population across the entire region.